Screenwriting
in the Land of Oz

Screenwriting
in the
Land
of
Oz

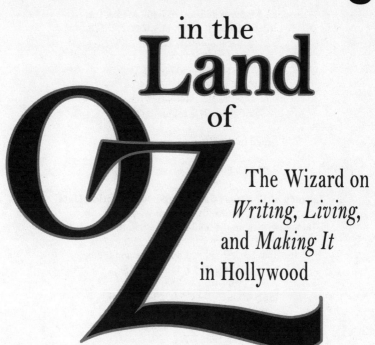

The Wizard on
Writing, Living,
and *Making It*
in Hollywood

RICHARD KREVOLIN

Introduction by Tom DeSanto,
producer of *Transformers* and *X-Men*

Foreword by Jeff Arch,
screenwriter of *Sleepless in Seattle*

Avon, Massachusetts

Published by
Adams Media, a division of F+W Media, Inc.
57 Littlefield Street, Avon, MA 02322. U.S.A.
www.adamsmedia.com

ISBN 10: 1-4405-0640-X
ISBN 13: 978-1-4405-0640-6
eISBN 10: 1-4405-0926-3
eISBN 13: 978-1-4405-0926-1

Printed in the United States of America.

10 9 8 7 6 5 4 3 2 1

Library of Congress Cataloging-in-Publication Data
Krevolin, Richard W.
Screenwriting in the land of Oz / Richard Krevolin.
        p.   cm.
Includes bibliographical references and index.
ISBN-13: 978-1-4405-0640-6
ISBN-10: 1-4405-0640-X
ISBN-13: 978-1-4405-0926-1 (e-book)
ISBN-10: 1-4405-0926-3 (e-book)
1. Motion picture authorship. I. Title.
PN1996.K7185 2011
808.2'3—dc22
2010039867

This publication is designed to provide accurate and authoritative information
with regard to the subject matter covered. It is sold with the understanding that
the publisher is not engaged in rendering legal, accounting, or other professional
advice. If legal advice or other expert assistance is required, the services of a
competent professional person should be sought.

—From a *Declaration of Principles* jointly adopted by a Committee of the
American Bar Association and a Committee of Publishers and Associations

Many of the designations used by manufacturers and sellers to distinguish their
products are claimed as trademarks. Where those designations appear in this book
and Adams Media was aware of a trademark claim, the designations have been
printed with initial capital letters.

This book is available at quantity discounts for bulk purchases.
For information, please call 1-800-289-0963.

**"Seeing *The Wizard of Oz*
made a writer of me."**

—SALMAN RUSHDIE

Acknowledgments

To Laura Daly, whose line editing helped bring this book to life.

To Joseph Bologna, who has been my Socrates.

To John Drdek and J. Michael Legat for their scene-writing skills.

To Sherman and Evelyn Krevolin for all their love and support.

To all my teachers and to all those students and writers I've had the privilege to teach.

And of course, to Paula, my editor, who consistently helped me along the yellow brick road on my way to the Emerald City.

Contents

Foreword

When Rich Krevolin asked me to write the Foreword for his book, *Screenwriting from the Soul*, I was happy and flattered and pleased to have the opportunity—not just to come through for Rich, but also because it gave me the chance to take a few things I had been thinking about, in the areas of writing and the writer's life in general, and see them published in a book that somebody else had already decided to publish and distribute, without any more effort required out of me.

I also saw it as a chance to have some fun, and I did have a lot of fun writing those pages. In fact, if I had the book in front of me right now, I'd be able to point out some of my favorite parts for you. However, as any experienced professional writer will tell you, when you're already in a very comfortable chair with your laptop strapped on, and you discover that the book you're referring to is not within direct arm's reach, which means you'd have to get up and do something about it if you actually want to refer to it, then maybe you're better off not referring to it after all, at least directly, because that could take you out of your chair—which leads me to two key things about writing that I feel are very important to pass on at this point:

1. Have a loyal and comfortable chair.
2. Stay in it.

Now you might be thinking, there's a word for what this guy is talking about, and that word is "lazy"—and all he's trying to do is justify his own laziness and call it "dedication" instead. To that I say, well maybe. I will freely admit that I'm not one of these guys you have to drag in from vigorous bouts of mountain climbing so that I can be forced to sit down and write. I would rather sit right here and climb my own mountains, so to speak, instead of the ones nature seems to always be putting outside somewhere, where you can pull your hamstrings off just breathing the air.

But also consider this—while I could have been up looking for that book, I got a lot more done on this Foreword instead, which brings me that much closer to finishing it. Whereas if I had gotten up, anything could have happened.

Of course, lots of times *good* things happen when you get up. In fact, the whole thing is a pretty tricky subject, so I'm just going to forget about it and move on ahead, to a time a few years later when Rich went and wrote another book about screenwriting, and asked me to write a Foreword for that one too.

Readers of *How to Adapt Anything into a Screenplay* might remember that this second request involved a free lunch at a great noodle house in L.A., which I happily slurped up, while Rich generously paid the tab.

And maybe it was the noodles, but one thing I remember about that second Foreword was that it ended up taking a pretty strong position on Giant Monster Puppets, which should motivate you right now to go and get Rich's second book, so you can see what the hell I was talking about. I would tell you myself, but *How to Adapt Anything . . .* is over on the same shelf as *Screenwriting from the Soul*—and as we've discussed earlier, both of those books are currently across the room. I, however, by staying in this chair, am maybe halfway through this Foreword by now, which is a good thing because (a) I have a lot of other work to do and (b) so do you.

I should say here, though, since this latest book of Rich's is gathered around *The Wizard of Oz*, that even if it means getting vilified for this, personally I did not like that movie, not one single bit. First of all because on just about every possible level, it freaked the crap out of me—just like it probably freaked the crap out of you, too, and everybody who ever saw it. But that doesn't mean I *wanted* to be freaked out, or that if I'd known ahead of time that I would be, I might have decided not to see it. I know it's supposed to be this big landmark thing and all, and it was—I'm just saying that I don't think there's one solid frame in that whole event that wasn't viscerally unpleasant to me and didn't make me wish I was watching something else. Something that wasn't a fricking nightmare everywhere you looked. Even though I get it that these are the things that made it so incredible, and incredibly important—the way it gets down into the absolute ground zero core psyche of your DNA and shakes it around like a golden retriever with a buttered rag doll in its mouth. In all its greatness, it was just way too disturbing, even if that's why it was so great. That movie made me so damn uncomfortable that I don't even want to talk about it anymore. I only brought it up because I figured I ought to.

Back to you then, and to Rich. If you're smart, you already have both of his earlier books, along with a deep bench of other good works—the kind that inspire you and inform you and help you make your way through all the highs and lows and in-betweens that go hand in hand with being a screenwriter, or any writer at all. In fact, even writers who never intended to try screenplays (there might be two of you) would benefit from reading these books anyway—because if nothing else, a good screenplay is all about storytelling and organized thinking and serious amounts of discipline. And every writer, no matter what he or she is writing, could stand to be better at those three things.

On the other hand, just ask anyone who knows a screenwriter if the words "organized thinking" and "serious discipline" are descriptions that readily come to mind when they think of this person. Because I'm fairly confident that most of us don't quite come off that way. Most of us are lucky if we successfully button our shirts before we go out somewhere. Some of us might even forget to *wear* a shirt—so, excuse the rest of the world for being surprised to learn that it takes serious discipline and organized thinking and major storytelling skills to be a good writer, based on the way most of us writers present ourselves to the public—that is, when we manage to go out at all.

Except maybe Truman Capote. Remember a few years ago when they made like nine movies about him, all at the same time? According to these movies, that little dude spent approximately 433 percent of his waking life being impeccably dressed and relentlessly attending classy social situations, talking in highly animated ways to very exciting people at the kind of glittery stimulating parties you and I will never get invited to—and yet he somehow found the time to turn out books that in some cases were so thick they needed their own zoning ordinances just to get an ISBN. Whereas the last party I was at featured something that might have been—*might* have been—chicken fingers. By that I mean that if chickens really had hands and someone decided to cut the fingers off of them, and dust them up with cornmeal and serve them raw to company, that is what this particular party treat looked like.

Here's the thing though. I could almost guarantee you that Truman Capote also saw *The Wizard of Oz,* and it probably freaked him out, too. In fact, if there's one thing that unites our entire culture, generations of it, it's that we have all been severely dysfunctionalized by that one same movie. From FDR to Obama, from Betty Grable to Madonna, from the girl who wins the gold in figure skating to the guy who flies the next plane you're on (think about *that* one)—if there are two singular traumas that all of us share, they are (1) the birth experience itself and (2) being screwed up for life because of that movie. After all, it is a known historical fact that one of the reasons George W. Bush invaded Iraq was, quote, "to get those damn flying monkeys out of my head." Not that therapy wouldn't have been a better choice or anything.

That's how powerful movies can be. Don't let anybody tell you different.

Anyway. One of the things I might have said in the Foreword to *Screenwriting from the Soul* (remember, it's all the way across the room and I'm still here in the chair) had to do with the difference between learning how to write and learning how to be the person who's doing the writing—and that where a lot of the other books lean more completely on the technical side, Rich's book covered both areas—and for that reason alone I thought you should buy it. I then went on to say what a great and decent human being Rich was, and still is—and not just because he asked me to write the Forewords for his first two books, and now this one, but because I've known him for a really long time now, personally and professionally, and I'm keen to get it across to you that here is someone that you could really stand to learn a lot from. Which is not grammatically the right way to say that, but you read it anyway so let's just keep going here.

Although I have to say to those of us whose grandparents had thick foreign accents and suffered unspeakable forms of indignity just to get to this country, though it was definitely important to them that their kids grew up and got proper educations and learned the difference between "who" and "whom," they also did it for a different, and larger reason—and that reason had nothing to do with pushing hand carts through Hell's Kitchen, or possibly being played by Mandy Patinkin one day, and everything to do with a little thing we like to call "freedom."

Which is where writing comes in. Because can you imagine writing without freedom? The freedom to write, and the freedom to write freely, about anything that matters to you, and in any form or manner you choose to write? Even the freedom to write *The Wizard of Oz*, if you happen to have that level of mean diabolical brilliance in you (but please don't). Of course, any responsible citizen will tell you—and by "responsible citizen," I don't mean those people in movie theaters who make more noise than a common advancing battalion and then tell you "it's a free country" and they can do anything they want to—I mean the other kind, who know that with "freedom" comes "responsibility"—the kind of person *you* are, who cherishes and appreciates this blessed First Amendment of ours, and the sacrifices that were made in its name. The kind that wants to go out there and *add* something, even if it's a ghoulish collective nightmare whose only positive element I can think of is that real estate in Kansas is still pretty affordable, measured against several comparable areas where that vicious terrifying movie did not take place.

Okay then. It's time to bring this thing around to the final fade. Time to finally get up out of this chair and get a couple other things done—a small delightful snack maybe, or a much-needed pit stop. And, what the heck—maybe I'll even go past that bookshelf and actually refer to the Forewords from Rich's other two books, although by now it's probably too late.

Then I'll come back to the chair and start writing again, because I've been doing this kind of thing for so long I pretty much don't know how to do anything else. But before I really do sign off here, I'd like to leave you with a few final things:

1. With the freedom to write comes the responsibility to take writing seriously. If you don't think I've been taking this Foreword seriously, even though I spent most of it goofing around, you are mistaken. I care about every word, and every piece of punctuation, almost more than it's sane to, and you should, too.

2. If you buy into #1, buy this book. Read it, mark it up, and take it to heart. Rich knows what he's talking about, he's been through the fire and here he is sharing his mojo with you. There are a lot of pieces to this puzzle, and you don't want to miss what you'd be missing if you think you can do without this one.

3. You damn well better care about the audience. They're trusting you with their time and money and a whole lot else. Care about them like nobody's business and they will reward you

like you can't believe. You should only write something that lasts as long and cuts so deep as the *Wizard*. I may not want to know about it, but I'll be happy for you.

4. Some people are born storytellers. There's really no way around it. The same way other people are born athletes, or performers or politicians. It happens. Rich even says, somewhere in this very book you're holding, that God whispers in certain people's ears for reasons only known to Him (or Her). If you're one of those, I say fantastic. Read #1 and #2 above anyway, and get better at the parts you're *not* so naturally good at. And then remember #3. Forget that one at your peril.

5. Truman Capote would probably be like a major fan of Twitter if he were alive right now. Don't you think? We could all know instantly what Tom and Rita are serving at their latest house party.

6. It would not be chicken fingers.

So that's it. The years have gone by since I first met Rich. I've been lucky to get a lot of time with him. We've laughed ourselves silly, copped to the things that we cry about, we've taught together, learned together, we've walked the streets of London at midnight, kayaked off Santa Barbara, we even did a Skype seminar once where Rich was in Hong Kong and I was at home, although it took six teenagers to show us how to do the Skype part. He's a great guy, a great teacher and one of the best and most caring friends you can find. And I know he would wish you everything I am wishing you now: that you earn your success and enjoy it.

You're a few pages closer to it already.

Follow your dreams, but keep your eye on the road. And may everything turn out just great. Just click your heels, three times . . .

Jeff Arch
No Place Like Home, California

Introduction

Some days writing feels like a house fell on you and someone tried to steal your shoes. But those are the bad writer block/procrastination/I should be writing but I'm watching *Oprah* days. Other days, however, writing is the tornado that lifts us out of our normal humdrum lives and magically transports us to our own personal Oz. This book will help make sure you are flying in the house and not crushed under it.

The only thing holding you back from writing and writing well is you. Like Dorothy, you always had the power within you but you just need to realize it and understand there really are no magic ruby red slippers. It is you and the blank page. How do you make the blank page the best it can possibly be? You need brains like the Scarecrow, a heart like the Tin Man, and courage like the Cowardly Lion.

The reason you bought this book is to become a better writer and make your dream a reality. Every writer starts out the same way, trying to escape our own reality, our "Kansas," and find that place where dreams in our head become the reality on the page. The one thing writing does take is work. There are two ways of writing: you can either work hard or work smart. Working smart is always better and a lot more fun and productive.

What Rich has done in his book is teach you how to work smart when you are writing. To get the most out of you, your time, and your talent. He passes along much sage advice like the Wizard. All with the goal of finding the magic of the story that is within you and helping you down your own story's yellow brick road. There will be pitfalls along that journey, but if you listen to the Wizard Rich Krevolin, you will avoid them.

Like the Tin Man's oil can, the lessons of this book will help grease the wheels if you get stuck. And any writer who has never been stuck is a person who lies about being a writer. Some days you won't need the oil, as the ideas will be flowing, but then you need to make sure what you are writing is good—does it have the

> **"A baby has brains, but it doesn't know much. Experience is the only thing that brings knowledge, and the longer you are on earth the more experience you are sure to get."**
>
> —L. FRANK BAUM,
> *THE WONDERFUL WIZARD OF OZ*

brains of the Scarecrow or are you just filling pages without knowing what you are writing toward.

Does your writing have a heart like the Tin Man? If your writing is all brains and no heart then no one will be invested emotionally. Using your heart will help you answer that all-important question of . . . do I care about these characters? Do I care about the story? If not, then you are not living up to your full potential as a writer, and the reader will be left cold.

Last and equally important is the need to have the Cowardly Lion's courage. The courage to tell the story you want to tell and to tell it well. To have the courage to listen to constructive criticism that this book offers, but still stay true to the voice of your story.

Dare to dream, and do yourself a favor and let Rich Krevolin's book help you make those dreams a reality.

Somewhere over the Rainbow,

Tom DeSanto,
Writer/Producer, *X-Men*,
Battlestar Galactica, Transformers

Prologue

Dear Reader,

I was lucky. I had a mentor. I called him Oz.

At the time, I didn't really think much about it. It's only now, years later, that I've come to realize how truly fortunate I was.

Let me explain. When I first started trying to write screenplays, I was lost and alone. It was a scary, frustrating time for me. I didn't know where to turn or what to do. In a blind, foolish panic, I reached out to a stranger, a veteran screenwriter whose work I was a fan of. Yep, I sent an e-mail to an old pro whom I'd never met but whose movies had changed my life. Hey, at that point in my life, I figured that I had nothing to lose. I mean, when you're that low, the only place to go is up, right?

He owed me nothing. I had never met him and he refused to allow me to pay him. But for some reason, he responded to all of my e-mails. He became my Wizard of Oz, and I, his Scarecrow, Tin Man, and Cowardly Lion. And eventually, that old pro reluctantly opened up to me and even became someone I could call "friend." Yes, I had found my teacher. Over the years, I irked, irritated, needled, cajoled, and flabbergasted him into sharing all the missteps he had made so that I could avoid making those very same mistakes. He gave me leeway as I grew as a writer, but he always clearly delineated guardrails so I would never veer too far off course.

And all the while, he taught me that everything you need to know about life and screenwriting can be found within the pages of L. Frank Baum's *The Wonderful Wizard of Oz*. It's true. Trust me, you'll see . . .

Screenwriting is a brutal, ridiculous calling. Sure, if you want to become a lawyer or a doctor, it's hard. It's a ton of work, but it can be done and once you've graduated from med school and/ or law school and passed all your exams, there are jobs out there. Thousands and thousands of positions. And there are people who need your services.

But screenwriting is different. There are hardly any openings for gainful employment, and if there are a few jobs, you must compete for them with established, Academy Award–nominated writers. Ouch!

As Oz said to me in one of his e-mails, "Being a writer is hard, being a professional writer is even harder, and being a working Hollywood screenwriter may be the hardest of all. But if you love stories—if you really, really love them—and more than anything else in the world, you want to write them . . . well, then, you must write." Ain't that the truth.

Yet as our relationship developed over the years, I came to see the sweet kindness that was hidden behind the rough gruffness. Oz might have been a bit of a cynic, but he also showed me that there was light at the end of the tunnel; an Emerald City at the end of every yellow brick road. Hope shall and must persist. The journey can be a lot easier if you have a friend, a guide, a torch that can help lead the way. For me, my light was always found in the words of this caring individual who returned my e-mails with his sage insights as to how I might navigate the treacherous seas of a screenwriting career.

In exercises and e-mails, I received the ultimate master class in screenwriting. Our correspondence was my film school, my MFA, my shortcut to becoming a professional screenwriter. In retrospect, he probably saved me ten years of struggling and heartache. (He'd probably tell me there is no such thing as a shortcut, but I believe his lessons surely saved me a lot of time and suffering.)

I spent a lot of time considering what would be the best way to sum up my decade-long interaction with my mentor. How do you organize a correspondence that occurred via e-mail sporadically over an entire decade?

How could I convey the wisdom of a great writer who is, well, let's just say a bit antisocial and who epitomized the statement, "Nobody is allowed to see the Wizard. Nobody. Ever!"

In the end, I decided that I really had no alternative. There really was no better way to capture the give and take, the ups and down, the blessings and curses of our relationship than to merely reprint the correspondence exactly as it occurred. So, the e-mails you'll see in this book are a verbatim, chronological record of our interaction. However, I do admit that certain aspects, such as dates, places, names, etc. have been changed or eliminated in order to protect the guilty. But in the end, none of that stuff really matters. What's really important is the content: his lessons and concepts and exercises that I've compiled for this book.

And let me acknowledge here and now that I still owe him a huge debt and I believe there really is no way to repay such a debt. The only thing I can imagine doing is this—to allow our correspondence to be published in book form so as to immortalize his life and words.

But enough throat-clearing. Let me get the hell out of your way.

All my best wishes for your future writing success,
Richard Krevolin

P.S. Oz once taught me that there really are only two different kinds of stories:

1. Those that start with a problem and end with a solution (a.k.a., comedies).
2. Those that start well and end badly (a.k.a., tragedies).

The story of my correspondence with Oz, the story that is captured via e-mail in the forthcoming pages, my story, our story, this story, the story of every writer finding his voice, is both comic and tragic. Thus, you will see elements of both comedy and tragedy in the following pages.

And let me just end by saying the following: may all my mentor's wisdom and generosity of spirit inspire you as a screenwriter to change the world for the better with your stories . . . and maybe even to shine a little light in places where once there was only darkness.

CHAPTER 1

Why Be a Screenwriter, Anyway?

Nobody is allowed to see the Wizard. NOBODY. EVER!

"Where are you all going?"

"To the Emerald City," said Dorothy, "to see the Great Oz."

"Oh, indeed!" exclaimed the man. "Are you sure that Oz will see you?"

"Why not?" she replied.

"Why, it is said that he never lets anyone come into his presence. I have been to the Emerald City many times, and it is a beautiful and wonderful place; but I have never been permitted to see the Great Oz, nor do I know of any living person who has seen him." ...

"That is very strange," said Dorothy; "but we must try, in some way, to see him, or we shall have made our journey for nothing."

—L. FRANK BAUM, *THE WONDERFUL WIZARD OF OZ*

From: "Dorothy" <WannaBeScribe@netmail.net>
To: "Oz" <OzProf@earthmail.com>
Subject: Please help . . .

Dear Professor Oz:

I am an aspiring writer in need of help, a sort of Dorothy, if you will, stuck in a Kansas-like state of mind. A Dorothy who is yearning for a twister to take her away, and in doing so help her find her Wizard of Oz and a happily-ever-after life in the Emerald City . . .

Okay, let me explain. I have always loved films (especially a few of the old ones that you wrote), and I know I can write movies that are better than the crap that Hollywood seems to be producing these days. I would love to go to film school, but I am really in no position to just get up, move, and go to school full-time right now. Especially with all the family and job-related stuff I'm dealing with right now. I'm sure you can appreciate my situation.

So here's the thing—I heard that sometimes screenwriting professors consult and I was wondering what your fees are like? I don't have a lot of money, but what little money I do have, I'd be happy to give to you if you could help make me into a real screenwriter.

Please say yes.

Sincerely Yours,
A Modern-Day Dorothy

P.S. I have included a copy of my most recent screenplay, which I was hoping you might be able to peruse at your earliest convenience.

From: "Oz" <ScriptProf@earthmail.com>
To: "Dorothy" <WannaBeScribe@netmail.net>
Subject: Please help . . .

Dear Dorothy:

1. I don't want your filthy money.

2. Stop labeling yourself as someone who is an aspiring screenwriter. If you are already writing scripts, then you are no longer aspiring, you are a screenwriter—maybe an unproduced screenwriter, but still, a real screenwriter. So please, stop aspiring, and keep writing.

3. I have downloaded the screenplay you attached and then I quickly and quietly tossed it into the recycle bin (trash) on my desktop. And rest assured, if you send me a hard copy, I will toss it into the cobalt blue Pacific Ocean where it belongs. RIP.

Best,
Oz

P.S. No one can make someone into a "real writer." You are either born with the curse or not. The reasons God chooses to whisper into the ear of one person and not another are known only to him.

P.P.S. I must admit, as a huge fan of *The Wonderful Wizard of Oz,* it was good to see that there are younger people out there today who are still fans of that wonderful, mythic story, which contains within its pages so many of the secrets of life.

What Is Your Motivation?

The first and single most important question that any writer must ask herself is this: Why write?

Why do you write? Why should anyone write? Why do some insist upon writing even though they know it will lead them to drink, divorce, or even insanity? Why try to become a screenwriter when it's so hard to ever get a movie made? Why bother when it's so much easier to watch TV or go to the movies? *Why write?*

One might as well ask, why breathe? Writers write because we can't help ourselves; writing keeps us from killing ourselves or others. And deep down in our souls, we write because we yearn to etch one tiny, seemingly insignificant scratch into the stainless-steel bones of culture; we fight, we persist, we persevere, we write; we are drawn to language like Romeo to Juliet. Throughout history, we find examples of this deeply human need to write, to record, to spin yarns, to create stories; and what better way to have your story told than in magnificent 3-D on a huge IMAX silver screen with booming Dolby THX surround sound!

For example, let's look at the life of one of the truly great and original voices of the past few hundred years—a pale, lonely Czech bureaucrat by the name of Franz Kafka. Kafka spent his life writing, yet in his last will and testament begged the executor of his estate to burn all of his work. Now, here's the rub: why didn't Kafka ensure that his work would never be seen by burning it himself?

The answer is simply this: As much as Kafka believed his writing to be worthless, there was something deep inside his soul that kept him from lighting the match. There was a part of him that desperately wanted to believe that maybe, just maybe, what he said might resonate with one person out there who was feeling the same pangs of terror and alienation that Kafka experienced on a daily basis. But mostly, Kafka couldn't help himself. He was a writer. No matter how inferior he believed his work to be, he kept on writing.

He wrote for himself; the tragic irony of his life is that he found his terrified and alienated audience only after his death.

Maybe you, like Kafka, are plagued with self-doubt. So, how do you go about discovering if what you write is any good, especially if you don't already have an established agent or producer who will read it? How can you find out if your words speak to others, if your work is not just the self-indulgent spouting of an ego yearning to be recognized, coddled, and loved?

In the end, there is no quick answer or final word. Writers prove themselves by doing one thing: they keep on writing. Professional writers spend a great deal of time trying to please others, but when you are starting out, write what you need and want to say. And if you have the bug, then my mentor's advice will, like the Muse, whisper in your ear, guide your fingers along the keyboard, and fill your mind with fresh characters and ideas.

One Upon a Time in Kansas

Everyone has a story to tell.

But being able to tell it well—to write it down in such a way that others want to pay you for the privilege of reading it or seeing it on the big screen—is indeed a rare occurrence. Writing well and structuring your story into an appealing and captivating narrative is a craft, one that can and should be honed over a period of years.

In fact, I would be lying if I told you that after reading this chapter, you would be able to write a perfectly executed, commercially viable Hollywood script. Even for most Hollywood insiders, screenwriting is a long, drawn-out process.

The development of your own particular voice is really what takes such a long time. Yet, rest assured, the years of work need not be a hardship; they can be tremendously rewarding. But if you're entering the writing game for fame and fortune, take my

A CAUTIONARY TALE FOR SCREENWRITERS

There once was a woman who wanted to be a dancer more than anything else in the world. From the time she could first walk, she went to dance classes. When she was eighteen, her boyfriend asked her to marry him and he said that he really wanted to settle down with her and have children. She loved him and wanted to do this. However, she also knew that if she got married, settled down, and had children, she would lose her prime dancing years and her dance career would be abruptly halted. Unsure of what to do, she decided to go see the artistic director of a famous dance company that was coming to town that weekend. She went to the dance venue, cornered the artistic director, and begged him to audition her. He agreed, and after watching her for ten seconds, he shook his head and said, "Sorry, but I don't think you have what it takes." With tears in her eyes, she bowed politely and exited. That summer, she got married and soon was pregnant. She never danced again.

However, years later, when her children were all grown, she read that the same dance company was coming to town once again and she went to see the show. When it was over, she snuck backstage and found the artistic director of the company, who was now very old. She approached him and said, "I'm sure you don't remember me, but more than twenty years ago, your company came to town and I auditioned for you and within a few seconds, you knew I didn't have it."

"Yes. So?"

"Well, my whole life I've always wanted to find out—how did you know so quickly?"

"Honey, if you let one person watch you dance for five seconds, and convince you that you don't have it, well, then, you really don't have it!"

advice right now and get out quick. Begone! Shoo! Take your stable income, your mortgage, your medical/dental plan, and scamper off to law school where you belong. Because there are positions all over the globe for well-trained lawyers and other service professionals, but there are only approximately seventeen people in the entire world who support themselves as full-time screenwriters. Okay, maybe 700 people, but still . . .

The thing is—every buffoon and his mother was trained to write in elementary school, so everyone believes that he can become a writer in his spare time. Believe it or not, it's the number one hobby in America. So be forewarned. The competition is fierce, and you'll face many roadblocks ahead.

There's No Place Like Hollywood

If you are one of the possessed writers whose life's dream is to write movies, then yes, you should be writing screenplays. As soon as you finish reading this book, write five screenplays and then throw them all away. But you argue, "Why should I toss them? Why shouldn't I submit them?" Because the truth is that until you have written a bunch of screenplays, you probably aren't ready to submit your work, especially to industry professionals.

Yet, still you argue, "Yes, it's my first screenplay, and it's not *Citizen Kane*, but it's still a whole heck of a lot better than most of the crap that seems to be coming out of Hollywood these days."

True, most of what Hollywood is producing these days is not very impressive; in fact, it seems as if the occasional well-written Hollywood film is more of a fluke than a commonplace occurrence. However, we must never forget that Hollywood's purpose is not and never has been to produce edifying pieces of art. Hence, it is called show *business*, not show *art*. If you want beauty, go to cosmetology school.

Exercise: Why Be a Screenwriter?

Let us start at the beginning with a little exercise in which you answer some basic questions about your desire to be a screenwriter.

- ❖ Who are you?
- ❖ What are you trying to achieve?
- ❖ Why are you even attempting to do this?
- ❖ What's your dream?
- ❖ Why do you have this primitive need to record your thoughts, to tell your stories, and to try to convey your dreams and desires, your personal experiences?
- ❖ What do you hope to gain by writing?
- ❖ Do you write to woo, shame, record, impress, flirt, hurt, thrill?
- ❖ Do you write to damage, pass the time, plumb the soul, narcotize, stimulate, or to transcend death, time, space?
- ❖ Do you write to create a thing of beauty, to become immortal?
- ❖ Specifically, why do you want to write screenplays?

What I need you to see from the very beginning is that this education is far more than a journey of learning a few scriptwriting techniques. This is a journey down the yellow brick road of self-knowledge; the act of writing a screenplay is the cyclone in which

"If you ever talk to anyone who has written, you'll always find a childhood in which, somewhere along the line, there's *Wizard of Oz*."

—WILLIAM STYRON

you will be tossed around. The journey is far longer than it seems, and you'll do many more revisions than you can ever imagine.

The Yellow Brick Road Awaits

Your first task is to start writing poignant, thought-provoking screenplays that come from your heart. And don't ever let anyone tell you that you can only write what you know. You can write anything you want as long as you write what you feel—from a deep, true place inside your soul.

From: "Dorothy" <WannaBeScribe@netmail.net>
To: "Oz"<ScriptProf@earthmail.com>
Subject: Here I am . . .

Dearest Wizard:

Whoa! I knew you were a bitter, jaded, cynical has-been, but I never dreamed you would have the nerve to tell me to consider law school instead. So let me just say up front, you are right; if I could go to law school, I would. But I want, I need, I have to write, and after having read your work, I have decided that you are the one who is going to teach me, whether you want to or not.

As one of your beloved Zen monks once said, "When the student is ready, the teacher shall appear and when the teacher is ready, the student shall appear."

So baby, here I am. Work with me!

Excited to learn,
Your most promising two-handed Tin Man

From: "Oz" <ScriptProf@earthmail.com>
To: "Dorothy" <WannaBeScribe@netmail.net>
Subject: Negatory . . .

> Dear Two-Handed Excited Young Tin Man:
> No. Sorry, but the answer remains—NO!
> Good luck finding your Zen master,
> Your favorite bitter, jaded, cynical, has-been HACK.
>
> P.S. Don't make me have to get a restraining order.

From: "Dorothy" <WannaBeScribe@netmail.net>
To: "Oz"<ScriptProf@earthmail.com>
Subject: C'mon, dude . . .

Dear Wizzie:

If you don't want to teach me, fine—this will be my last letter. But you should know that the movie and playscripts you wrote have made a difference, at least in my life, and that is why I so desperately want to work with you. But if you are not up to it, I understand and will have to respect your wishes.

I remain,

Your biggest fan

P.S. More specifically, since we are never going to correspond again, I thought you should know that a few years ago I read a tattered, dog-eared copy of one of your old plays which I bought for a nickel at a garage sale. It affected me so deeply that I sent my father a copy; he read it, called me up, and we spoke for the first time in many years. I know that my personal life is probably of no concern to you, but your writing brought me closer to my dad before he died and that is why I am forever indebted to you.

So, whatever your choice, I understand your desire for privacy and will attempt to abide by your wishes.

CHAPTER 2

Enter the Writing Cyclone

It is fortunate for Kansas that you have no brains.

"Tell me something about yourself, and the country you came from," said the Scarecrow, when she had finished her dinner. So she told him all about Kansas, and how gray everything was there, and how the cyclone had carried her to his queer land of Oz. The Scarecrow listened carefully, and said,

"I cannot understand why you should wish to leave this beautiful country and go back to the dry, gray place you call Kansas."

"That is because you have no brains," answered the girl. "No matter how dreary and gray our homes are, we people of flesh and blood would rather live there than in any other country, be it ever so beautiful. There is no place like home."

The Scarecrow sighed.

"Of course I cannot understand it," he said. "If your heads were stuffed with straw, like mine, you would probably all live in the beautiful places, and then Kansas would have no people at all. It is fortunate for Kansas that you have no brains."

—L. FRANK BAUM, *THE WONDERFUL WIZARD OF OZ*

From: "Oz" <OzProf@earthmail.com>
To: "Dorothy" <WannaBeScribe@netmail.net>
Subject: Okay, okay already . . .

Dear Biggest Fan:
A nickel? Even in piss-poor condition, my play's a collector's item worth at least twenty bucks. You've obviously got a good head for bargains.

You know, I had no idea that anyone out there really cared about my work, let alone that it has effected such dramatic, positive change in the lives of others. Thank you for sharing your story with me; it means far more to me than you could ever imagine. I am moved by your passion and will reconsider your proposition.

In other words, so-o-o, where do you want to start?

With loving affection,
Your hero,
The Dramatic Writing Wizard

P.S. If you want to learn, I'll teach; but please, let us keep my private life out of the mix. Thank you very much.

From: "Dorothy" <WannaBeScribe@netmail.net>
To: "Oz" <OzProf@earthmail.com>
Subject: Let us begin

Dear Dramatic Writing Wizard:
I understand and will respect your desire for privacy.

Okay, then, let us start at the beginning—you know, with the fundamentals, and then go from there, okay?

Eagerly Awaiting the Education of My Life,
Your numero uno acolyte

What Is Storytelling?

The act of creating a story is really the act of trying to figure out how to put forward a theme or a moral position in such a way that it is buried within a narrative that is engaging and compelling. And if this is done right, no one will notice that you are also really putting forth your *personal* moral agenda, your take on the difficult questions of being alive, your belief in the human capacity for change; they will just sit back and enjoy the story you are telling them.

In truth, the journey of writing a screenplay never ends. Even as the last shot fades out and the movie ends, there are always sequels to write. After all you learn in this book, I hope you will come to see that it's not just about a sale, but also about the development of your characters' arcs as well as your own character. The journey is the thing, the path is the goal; the act of creation is significant and valuable in and of itself. Personal fulfillment and happiness are simply the byproducts of all of your creative endeavors. But remember: in the end, one writes stories to learn and to further one's own growth as a human being. That is all.

Taking Off for (Inner) Parts Unknown: Beyond Obsession

Let us look for a moment at a Hollywood comedy that is still one of my favorites, *Mrs. Doubtfire*. Daniel, the main character, played by Robin Williams, is forced to deal with the many complications that result from him trying to lead a dual life. Seventy-nine minutes into this movie (I'm sorry, I time movies; it's my job), Daniel, in despair, screams out to the world, "What am I doing here? This is *beyond obsession!*"

And this is where I want to start: obsession. I am not just talking about mere ordinary obsession; I'm talking about being *beyond obsession*. That is the only mindset that will serve as a foundation for a person who wants to be a working writer in a world that is not designed to foster artistic growth and change but only to perpetuate stereotypical sameness and mass consumption.

Once you are ready to live a life beyond obsession, you're ready to begin your Hollywood education. One day, you may even sell something you have written. And then, years after your death, like Kafka, you may even achieve a modicum of fame. Maybe . . .

 ## STORIES ARE FLUID

Stories are essential, but they are also always in flux; they need to be readjusted and tweaked, and, once in a while, new and original tales need to be created to ease our way through transitional moments.

Storytelling is a part of us, programmed deep within our DNA. Look at the ancient cave paintings in Lascaux, France. They are not simply portraits. They are a series of action-based images, the first "movies—the first recorded signs of man's need to tell stories, to empower himself and perpetuate his race. His survival hinged upon it. Simply put, if caveguy number one could convey to caveguy number two how he killed the animal that was his primary source of nourishment, he teaches others and helps his children start from a better place than he did. Stories give us a proverbial "leg up" and represent the building blocks of society. Progress, forward motion, human betterment—they are all stories we tell ourselves and each other.

Telling Everyone's Story

Like every other screenwriter, you want to tell the world your story. Yet consider this: your story is also universal. Viktor Frankl, in his seminal post-Holocaust work, *Man's Search for Meaning*, demonstrated convincingly that man cannot survive without a reason for living, or a personal narrative that provides him with meaning.

In this act of telling your story, of dramatizing your specific tale, you have the potential to transcend the individual, to speak to society as a whole and touch their souls. In other words, the story of one person, told well, can speak to and resonate with us all. Shakespeare's tale of *King Lear* is the story of a historical figure, a real individual who once lived, but it is also the tale of every father and daughter—a tale that still speaks to us—across generations and centuries. So, when you tell your story, you are actually telling the story of all humanity, and sometimes even endowing life with meaning and a sense of the divine.

Types of Story Structures

Everything begins with the impulse to tell a story. This is not a luxury, but an essential part of our genetic makeup. People need stories. They give us a context; they locate us within ourselves, our society, and our global village. In some cultures, a person's story is considered his greatest treasure, his most sacred resource. Without stories, how would we live? We develop personal and cultural mythologies to help us lead our lives. Consider this: the most significant Western cultural myth of the past 2,000 years is the story of a truly special historical figure: Jesus. But what exactly is the best storytelling form? Here are two of the most popular structures used in screenplays.

ARISTOTELIAN STRUCTURAL

Thousands of years ago, a smart guy in a toga named Aristotle studied stories and came up with some rules about structure. Since human beings are essentially the same as they were a few thousand years ago, I would argue that what Aristotle came to believe about stories still applies today. So let's start there, with Aristotelian structural guideposts.

In his *Poetics*, Aristotle talked about how all stories must have a beginning, a middle, and an end (three acts) in which a protagonist journeys through "a series of experiences which leads to a climactic moment toward the end where he learns something, discovers something about himself that he could have known all along but was blind to. This discovery must be incredibly emotionally powerful. This revelation should change the entire course of the protagonist's life—*and that change should be for the better. The protagonist should learn, grow, develop, become a better person and as a result, society is enriched.* Unless, of course, the story is a tragedy and then this discovery occurs, but it tragically occurs too late.

THE CLASSICAL STRUCTURE

The classical story structure, on the other hand, mimics life and nature:

- ✧ Act I—Birth, spring, innocence, vitality
- ✧ Act II—Summer and fall, maturation and disillusionment
- ✧ Act III—Winter, death, despair

And sometimes, there is an epilogue or
- ✧ Act IV—a new spring, rebirth, resurrection

This general structure is another one you can think about as you imagine your story told in a screenplay format.

In Simple Form: Cyclone, Oz, Back to Kansas

Here's another way to think of a story structure. In a nutshell, start your story with an apparently stable status quo that is disturbed by a catalyst (the cyclone) that sends things into a state of flux, transition, and disorder. As a result of this chaos, new elements are formed, which allow for transformation and change (the Wizard of Oz). This chaos inevitably leads to a new state of equilibrium that is similar to, yet different from, the original status quo (Dorothy goes back to Kansas).

The Oz's Golden Rule of Storytelling

Of course, Oz himself has a storytelling rule of his own:

> *An engaging character actively overcomes tremendous obstacles to reach a desirable goal, and in doing so, he or she changes for the better.*

This is a non-negotiable paradigm. I think you would be hard-pressed to find a great story that does not follow this rule. And note the emphasis on *change* and *betterment*. Nobody wants to pay $14 for a movie ticket or $125 for a theater ticket to see something that they can see on the street for free.

Viewers Want to See Betterment

When we include the word *betterment* in the definition of storytelling, we see that writing is a highly moral act. True, there are cases where betterment comes too late, or never comes—such as in unconventional tragedies like *Midnight Cowboy*, *Thelma & Louise*, *Million Dollar Baby*, *Schindler's List*, *Titanic*, and even *The Godfather II*, which features the unforgettable final image of

"True art clarifies life, establishes models of human action, casts nets toward the future, carefully judges our right and wrong directions, celebrates, and mourns. It does not rant. It does not sneer or giggle in the face of death, it invents prayers and weapons. It designs visions worth trying to make fact. It does not whisper or cover or throw up its hands and bat its lashes . . . . It strikes lightning or *is* lightning."

—JOHN C. GARDNER, *ON MORAL FICTION*

Michael Corleone sitting alone in his glass office while the sound of his brother being shot echoes through his mind, forever. Yet even these tragedies are, at their cores, highly moral. And most stories in post–Reagan era Hollywood are not tragedy but "hero myths," what the Greeks would call comedies. That is, they're stories driven by our need for eternal redemption and happy endings.

The reality of our lives is simply that we yearn for betterment because most people don't change. Your uncle is the same stubborn bastard that he was ten years ago, and he will probably go to the grave that same stubborn bastard. That's why Hollywood hasn't bothered to option the rights to your uncle's life. However, if your uncle's a stubborn bastard who learns, who changes—if he's the grand dragon of the Ku Klux Klan who falls in love with his Latina maid, learns she's infertile, then adopts forty Mexican orphans and ends up becoming a Cesar Chavez type, leading the movement for reform of the conditions of Latino migrant workers—now that's a story I'll gladly part with ten bucks to see.

After all, we go to the theatre or the movie house to sit in a dark womb with a bunch of strangers and vicariously experience this human transformation. Like the Greeks, for whom theater was a communal and religious gathering wherein the fears and desires of the culture could be exorcised and expressed, modern-day plays and movies let us come together to create a new sense of the community we have lost to technology and current lifestyles.

Humans want to grow, and we will pay to see the transformation of other human beings. By watching someone experience an epiphany and change, I too am transformed. All in two hours for a mere ten bucks, while most therapists charge at least $150 an hour.

ESSENTIAL EPIPHANIES

But, c'mon now, is it really necessary to have this change, this epiphany, by the end of the story?

Yes. No character arc, no change, no movie.

As for epiphanies, they are the heart and soul of any worthwhile tale; they are inherently linked to good storytelling. Without them, just forget about it—pack up your things, turn your computer off, and start again some other day.

And so, let me reiterate my golden rule, since this is so fundamental, so basic and important to the telling of a good story:

An engaging character actively overcomes tremendous odds to reach a desirable goal, and in doing so, he or she changes for the better.

"[An epiphany is] a sudden spiritual manifestation whether in the vulgarity of speech or of gesture or in a memorable phrase of the mind itself. It is for the artist to record these epiphanies with extreme care, seeing that they themselves are the most delicate and evanescent of moments." —JAMES JOYCE

The Four Directions of Oz

Let me elaborate my golden rule even further. There are certain essentials you need to tell a story that movie-going audiences will want to see: a goal, obstacles, motivation, and a conclusion.

1. TRUE NORTH (THE GOAL)

Your main character must have a strong goal. Without being overly reductive, don't forget to ask yourself, "What does my main character want?" The goal must be an expression of an inner need the character has. Establish specific personality traits that distinguish this character from any other. These traits are what make him memorable and quirky, and they help explain why his goal is what it is. Make your main character someone who is so engaging that viewers can connect to him. He doesn't have to be the nicest person in the world, as long as he and his goal are inherently interesting. I wouldn't want Tony Soprano or *Taxi Driver*'s Travis Bickle as my friend or relative (in fact, I don't really even like them), but heck, they are compelling, and I want, I care, I need to see what happens to them.

2. EAST (OBSTACLE)

What or who is keeping our protagonist from achieving his goals? Those obstacles will help provide the action and plot points of your story.

3. SOUTH (MOTIVATION)

Why do your characters want what they want? This is the stuff that is going on inside that drives them, and you must find a way to illustrate this motivation externally.

4. WEST (CONCLUSION)

How, in the end, do your characters achieve or fail to achieve their goal? Does it happen in a surprising, unexpected way? Wrapping up your story will answer these questions.

From: "Dorothy" <WannaBeScribe@netmail.net>
To: "Oz" <OzProf@earthmail.com>
Subject: More, more, more . . .

Dear Wizzie Baby:
Wow! Under that cranky, prehistoric veneer is a brilliant, learned human being. Who would have thought? I love it, but need a bit of time to process it all. Will write back soon.
Thanks a million,
Your Scarecrow

CHAPTER 3

If You Only Had a Writer's Brain

If Oz will not give you any brains,
you will be no worse off than you are now.

"Who are you?" asked the Scarecrow when he had stretched himself and yawned, "and where are you going?"

"My name is Dorothy," said the girl, "and I am going to the Emerald City, to ask the great Oz to send me back to Kansas."

"Where is the Emerald City?" he inquired. "And who is Oz?"

"Why, don't you know?" she returned, in surprise.

"No indeed. I don't know anything. You see, I am stuffed, so I have no brains at all," he answered sadly.

"Oh," said Dorothy, "I'm awfully sorry for you."

"Do you think," he asked, "if I go to the Emerald City with you, that the great Oz would give me some brains?"

"I cannot tell," she returned, "but you may come if you like. If Oz will not give you any brains, you will be no worse off than you are now."

"That is true," said the Scarecrow.

—L. FRANK BAUM, *THE WONDERFUL WIZARD OF OZ*

From: "Dorothy" <WannaBeScribe@netmail.net>
To: "Oz" <OzProf@earthmail.com>
Subject: More, more, more . . .

Dear Highly Esteemed Wiz:
Okay, have read your last e-mail over and over again and all I can say is—more, more, more! Can you be specific in terms of screenplay format? Pretty please, with Stevia on top. Also, which books should I read as a supplement to my education?
Awaiting your next entry,
Your Most Subservient Scarecrow

P.S. I know you don't want to talk about your personal life, and I respect that; however, since I'm a highly visual person, I'd appreciate a recent photo of you. All I've ever seen is an old snapshot from *Who's Who*. It doesn't have to be professional, just some image of you that I can have when I imagine you lecturing to me.

From: "Oz" <OzProf@earthmail.com>
To: "Dorothy" <WannaBeScribe@netmail.net>
Subject: You asked for it . . .

Dear Scarecrow:
Rest assured, if you keep at this writing thing, what you will find is all the straw in your head will turn into fodder for good scripts. With regard to my recent physical appearance, just think about what God might look like, and there you have it . . . Think Morgan Freeman, only taller.
Signed,
Clean & Godly

First Things First

I used to lecture at many writers' conferences and what always amazed me was that most of the attendees seemed obsessed with all the wrong things. They would inevitably ask about agents and fees and contracts—yet these are the last things a beginner writer should be thinking about. All that stuff will come to the forefront one day once you have mastered your craft, but if you focus on it early in your career, you probably won't actually *have* a career as a professional writer.

The key thing to focus on as you are starting is merely this: good writing. Learn how to turn a sentence so that it sings. Learn how to tell a story well so that it engages an audience. Learn how to become invisible so it is always about the story and not you. These are essential skills that take years, if not decades, to master, so forget all that stuff about agency commission and standard writing fees and focus on your *art*!

Brain Food for Screenwriters

The easiest way to start becoming a better writer is to read really good writers. What amazes me when I meet people who want to be good writers is the fact that so few of them read! It's a simple fact that to be a good writer you need to be an avid reader. Yes, reading *can* make a difference; yet, no matter how many books you read, the key to becoming a better writer lies in the disciplined and monotonous practice of putting one's buttocks into a seat and writing. However, since it is unhealthy to write all day long, there should be time allotted for family and loved ones (note, these may be different people), food, sleep, sex (hopefully?), movie-watching, and the reading of certain books that may prove to be inspiring and edifying.

WORKS OF LITERATURE

The following represents a Whitman's Sampler of works of literature that you ought to be familiar with.

If you want to see how to write a good, clean, clear, honest sentence, read Charles Bukowski. If your writing lacks a certain poetic flair, revisit a great poet's work, such as Robert Frost or Walt Whitman. If your sentences are falling flat and feel too short, dwell in the luxurious, elegant prose of T. Coraghessan Boyle, John Cheever, or John Updike (wherein you'll find the secrets to life). If your writing seems to be falling flat, go back to Faulkner; if your sense of the absurd seems to be on the wane, go to *Without Feathers* by Woody Allen; to help you write concise, powerful screenwriterly stage descriptions, go straight to Raymond Chandler.

Plunge into Stephen Hawking's writings on the universe. Pore over Diane Ackerman's books *A Natural History of the Senses* and *A Natural History of Love*. Study all the Nobel Prize for Literature acceptance speeches, especially William Faulkner's. Analyze C.G. Jung, Joseph Campbell, and all the Native American myths you can get your hands on. Peruse Harold Goddard's two books on the works of Shakespeare, and then go back and read Shakespeare again.

BOOKS VERSUS MOVIES

While you're doing all this reading, please think about the differences and similarities between books and their movie adaptations. In other words, look at film adaptations and see what the screenwriters chose to keep and what they changed. Most importantly, try to understand why they made the choices they did. Film is a visual medium and novels are a psychological medium, so they have different demands and requirements. You can learn a tremendous amount by comparing and contrasting them.

Take, for example, the death of the Wicked Witch of the West. In L. Frank Baum's original novel, the scene has Dorothy getting mad because the witch steals one of her silver shoes (yep, in the book they are silver slippers, not ruby—silver did not look good on film, so the wizards at MGM changed the shoes to red). Baum writes, "This made Dorothy so very angry that she picked up the bucket of water that stood near and dashed it over the Witch, wetting her from head to foot."

Now, in the MGM film, it's a bit different. Dorothy throws the bucket of water at the Witch not in anger, but to save her beloved friend, the Scarecrow. Same scene, different story elements . . . and a very smart move by the screenwriters who altered it. Dorothy's actions become more powerful and moving to the audience because they are motivated by a higher emotion—love—instead of a baser emotion—anger.

READ IT AND WRITE

There is a plethora of so-called writing handbooks—some are better than others. Read as many as you can, gleaning gems of wisdom in each that you feel you can apply directly to the specific genre or style in which you are writing. Among some of my personal favorites are:

- ✧ *Poetics* by Aristotle
- ✧ *Writing Screenplays That Sell* by Michael Hauge
- ✧ *Screenwriting: The Art, Craft, and Business of Film and Television* by Richard J. Walter
- ✧ *Bird by Bird* by Anne Lamott
- ✧ *Theory and Technique of Playwriting* by John Howard Lawson (almost impossible to find, but well worth any price)
- ✧ *The Tools of Screenwriting* by David Howard & Edward Mabley

✧ *The Writer's Journey* by Christopher Vogler
✧ Anything by Dr. Linda Seger
✧ *Letters to a Young Poet* by Rainer Maria Rilke

Go to your local public library and take out books on subjects that you are unfamiliar with. For example, if you want to be a screenwriter, take out great works of nonfiction, or poetry, or architecture. Force yourself to think about more than movies and what you might find is that the movies you start writing seem more incisive, deeper, and more intelligent.

 # THE MOZART EFFECT FOR SCREENWRITERS

If you like to write with music playing in the background, I suggest you listen to Aretha Franklin, Simon & Garfunkel, Sammy Davis Jr., Ella Fitzgerald, Jackson Browne, Rebbesoul, Van Morrison, Barbra Streisand, Sarah Mclachan, Tom Petty, Neil Young, Cat Stevens, Dylan, Dan Bern, Enya, Springsteen, and literate show tunes such as the soundtracks to *Title of Show*, *Les Miserables*, and *Next to Normal*. Avoid Andrew Lloyd Webber and anything grungy, alternative, or techno. (Notice that I haven't listed many recent artists listed. This is simply a function of the fact that I am an old fart and I believe that most of the recent music that you hear on the radio is really a rehashing of the great artists of the past.) Cover the walls of the room you write in with paintings by Chagall, Klimt, and Gauguin, for these artists will inspire your soul to soar.

Movies to Watch

For inspiration while you write your screenplay, watch:

- ✧ Every movie starring Charlie Chaplin, Buster Keaton, Harold Lloyd, and Wallace & Gromit for comedic inspiration
- ✧ The work and films of Joseph Bologna and Rudy Deluca, two modern-day masters of comedy
- ✧ Jeff Arch's romantic comedies
- ✧ The action-adventure films of Tom DeSanto
- ✧ Ingmar Bergman's films, but not when you're depressed (they often deal with despair)
- ✧ Quentin Tarantino films for violent black comedies—but skip anything he has done since *Pulp Fiction* until *Inglourious Basterds*
- ✧ The work of Preston Sturges, Alfred Hitchcock, and Stanley Kubrick, for a look at quality classic films

Get these great films on DVD and study them. Watch them over and over, analyzing how the scenes are put together. In what order is information revealed? What do these films show and not show? In other words, what is put on the screen and what is left off-screen? When is the main character introduced and how? What does the main character want throughout the story? How does the director's hand seem present, but also invisible? Watch movies on large screens whenever you can, to get the full effect the screenwriters and directors intended. Look for large multiplex theaters, where you can sneak around and see two or three films in an evening (avoid getting caught, of course).

TRAVEL, BUT ...

Go ahead, travel around the world—and then come back home to realize that everything you need is already there. Emily Dickinson never left her house. Artist Marc Chagall lived all over the world, but his canvases all emerged from his childhood and his childlike soul.

Listen to the Words of Oz

When all else fails, get ahold of audiobooks (fiction, nonfiction, it doesn't matter, just make sure you are listening to great stories and mind-altering writing that is appropriate for the genre you are working on. So, for example, if you are writing a great detective screenplay, listen to every detective novel of the master, James Lee Burke). Continue to listen as you exercise each day. Play audiobooks in your car and surround yourself with language while you idle away the hours in traffic. But please, make sure you listen to the appropriate audiobook at the appropriate time. Raymond Carver's short stories are wonderfully dense, but if your desire is to bring your screenplay or stage play to life with luxurious language, Carver represents a poor choice to emulate.

Where to Write

When it comes to penning a screenplay, home is the best place to be. It's likely where you're most at ease and where you have access to the comforts that will help you write effectively. Comfort foods, a hot cup of coffee or tea, the right tunes, soft lighting, wifi, you name it—it is usually available in your house and so please establish your safe sanctuary in which the words can flow forth.

Avoid writing in public places, especially coffee houses (way too artsy-fartsy).

Keep Your Writing Simple

Above all else, your writing should be easy to read. Writing for the screen is different than writing for an English composition class; there is no need to impress with the literary quality of your prose. In fact, overwriting is a major sin in screenwriting, and in many cases, full sentences aren't even necessary . . . Which leads us to the hirsute beast known as style.

Essentially, a screenplay should consist almost entirely of action verbs and nouns, with very few adjectives and hardly any adverbs. The only information that appears should be that which facilitates the reader's visualization of your story concept. Everything else should be edited out.

A caveat: If you read many of the screenplays that are sold today, you'll see cutesy asides that are made specifically to the reader of the screenplay—information that could never make it onto the screen (like smells or inner psychological stuff). This is a stylistic choice and if you believe it will add pleasure to the reading experience, throw it in, but be advised: screenwriting is not a literary form. You don't have to be Saul Bellow, and no one will care about your use of metaphors.

"To be, is to be perceived."

—BISHOP BERKELEY

The Courage to Tell the Truth

In the end, screenwriting simply comes down to this:

The Writer's and Reader's Contract of Truth

Writer: I am going to tell you the truth.
Reader: I am going to believe you, I am going to connect with you, marry you, and suspend my disbelief, but I am only one false line of dialogue or unmotivated action away from reestablishing my disbelief and instantly divorcing you. I am always thinking, could this really happen? Does this story satisfy me intellectually, emotionally, viscerally? Does it move me? Touch me? Where? How? Remember above all, film is a visual and visceral medium, *not a verbal or cerebral one. Don't tell me, show me with riveting images.*

Show your audience (don't tell them) what they need to know, and they will follow you anywhere.

Despite a screenwriter's best efforts, there are still times when the story seems to fail, when something about it does not ring true. This pulls me out of the story, snaps me out of my trance, and forces me to think, "Hey! Wait a second. C'mon now, this couldn't happen!" When this occurs, the writer has failed to obey the basic rules of the world. For example, if there are aliens in your movie, fine, but you must hint of their existence early. You can't just have aliens show up in the last ten minutes out of nowhere to save the day. In other words, *aliens ex machina* is a big no-no. Crucial elements must be planted early and brought to fruition later.

The penalty for not sowing and cultivating the seeds of believability early and often first became clear to me when I used to watch movies with my mother. Whenever we'd be sitting in a movie theater or at home in front of the television, and a hole in the story appeared, she would always slap me on the shoulder and say, "C'mon! That would never happen. That's stupid, right?!"

And you know what? She was always right. Even though she wasn't a writer, she intuitively sensed a problem in the story. You see, when the writer's hand becomes visible in its efforts to cover gaping holes, and as a result we see action or hear dialogue that does not fit into the story's scheme or is inconsistent with the characters as established, we are disturbed, and rightfully so. Action must flow and not just occur to further the plot. In other words, *if it ain't organic, it ain't allowed.* You must control your characters instead of letting them control you.

The parameters of your world can include anything, but once they are established, they may not be broken, or else your audience will feel like they're getting a good jab in the ribs. And we all know how much audiences want to be stroked, not jabbed!

A good story should grab the reader immediately and keep her turning the page. Every development person in Hollywood has stacks of screenplays to get through and is dying to find a reason not to finish yours. Don't give them one.

The Heart of the Inexperienced Writer

As a neophyte writer, you have an arduous journey ahead. Yet, your lack of literary notoriety and success can be reframed into a blessing.

You have the obligation and the freedom to create your own mythology. Take it seriously; it is no easy task. Be justifiably intimidated by its burden, and then rise to the occasion by telling great stories that elevate men and women rather than downsize them; that speak of the greatness of humanity, not of its pettiness; that talk of the potential of human nature for redemption and transformation, not shallowness and stagnation; that urge us to strive to greater heights instead of the lowest common denominator. Have your characters lead us to the knowledge that we are no longer destined to repeat the mistakes of the past. Give us characters that beg us to constantly reinvent ourselves in new lights, cleaner, clearer, purer halogen bulbs that illuminate the good way, the just and right way.

So now, as you search for a place to enter the untamed screenwriting forest, don't settle for a well-trodden path. Don't settle down; don't settle in; don't settle.

Someone has to blaze trails. Someone is destined to be the voice of the twenty-first century; why not you? Write as if your voice can and will make a difference, and what you might find is that one day, just maybe, you *will* be hailed as the voice of the next era.

To become this voice, don't hoard your best material. Squander it. Now.

Put your best foot forward. It is harder to break in than it is to stay in. Use all your best lines and scenes now. Don't worry. When you are ready to write your next piece, you will have accumulated more material. And by that time, you will probably be obsessed by many other important new themes.

 ## LEAVE THE DIRECTING TO THE DIRECTOR

Note that very few camera angles are specified. Remember, you are not the director. You are merely the writer, the architect, the drawer of the blueprint upon which the movie will be based. Yes, you're the creative genius—the mastermind behind it all, and without you nothing would be possible—but still, yours is not to choose which camera angle will be used in what situation. Give only as much information as you must to create a series of stunning images in the mind's eye of your reader.

Let your voice reverberate in the dark night and never, I repeat, never remain silent. That is the cardinal sin of the writer. Speak, let your voice ring true and listen for the echo, the ramifications of your words. And if you are truly speaking from your marrow, you will see that your language resonates in the bones of all mankind. Write, let your words sing, and then sit back, cross your fingers, and pray that your story resonates deeply with your audience. You can do nothing more and there is nothing else that is more valuable to your own growth as well as that of all people.

Don't Stop Writing

Sure, even the best writers run into roadblocks and need breaks to recharge their batteries, but if you just keep working, you will never dry up like a riverbed during a drought. Keep working and the words will keep coming. Trust me on this one. Keep writing; the act of writing itself is the key. It should become the central focus, safe haven, and metaphor of your life. Remember, the difference between writers and people who write is the difference between bullfighters and bullshitters.

It's the Formatting, Dorothy

Now comes the boring but still essential point: If you want to be a professional writer, your work should look as if it were written by a professional. This means using proper screenplay format. If you have the money to buy them, there are many software programs designed to help you format your work. I use a program called Final Draft and love it.

If you don't have the money to buy a separate program, you can use the tabs and formatting options on your computer's word processing software (or typewriter, if you're using one!). Either way, you need to know how your pages should look. As an example, I have reprinted the first page of an old screenplay of mine that should serve as a suitable model. (Since it dealt with substantial historical, political, and cerebral issues, it was, of course, never made.)

Note that the font is twelve-point Courier. The margin needs to be larger (one and a half inches) on the left side to accommodate the binding, which should be a single round-head brass fastener in each of the three holes. This method *is* old-school, but it continues to be the standard. However, today, most scripts are e-mailed as PDF files, so many times there is no need to print it at all. Formats do differ, but in general, there should be four comfortable margins (at least one inch wide) and most scripts average around fifty-two lines per page. I recommend using Final Draft brand software to help with your formatting, but you can also create your own style sheet with Microsoft Word.

From: "Dorothy" <WannaBeScribe@netmail.net>
To: "Oz" <OzProf@earthmail.com>
Subject: And away we go in your beautiful balloon . . .

Dear Formatting Wiz:
This is all good stuff. Many thanks. Now can you give me an exercise I might do to try to implement all of your helpful hints?
Eagerly awaiting a difficult assignment,
Dorothy

FADE IN --

EXT. TROTSKY'S HOUSE/FORTRESS, MEXICO CITY -- DAY

A concrete-walled fortress on Avenida Vienna in Coyoacan,
Mexico. A quaint Mexican street in which the only noise is the
sound of chirping birds.

INT. TROTSKY'S FORTRESS — DAY

Inside the concrete walls is Trotsky's garden filled with
trees, cactus, flowers, pre-Columbian Aztec sculptures, and
singing birds. There is one large iron gate, which connects
the outside world to this idyllic inner sanctum.

On the left is a hutch filled with rabbits. Exotic wire cages
filled with colorful chirping birds hang from the trees. Along
the far left wall is a black tripwire.

On the right is a door leading into a living/dining room. A
story above the living/dining room is Trotsky's study and bal-
cony, which looks out over the garden.

In the center of the garden a young Mexican girl, SILVIA,
16, cradles the limp body of LEON TROTSKY, 60, who has bloody
white sheets wrapped around his wounded head. Trotsky's wife,
NATASHA SEDOVA, 60, watches in horror.

Silvia takes Trotsky's hand and holds it against her chest.
Trotsky begins to shiver and his teeth chatter.

                    TROTSKY
          It's so cold . . .

Silvia holds him close to her chest, like a mother cradling
her newborn child.

                    MATCH DISSOLVE TO:

THE GARDEN -- MANY YEARS LATER —

The CAMERA pulls back to reveal that Silvia is now in her mid-
thirties, and the years have not been kind to her.

                    SILVIA (V.O.)
          It is 1962. Late August. The time when the
          big breeze blows over the mountains . . .

CHAPTER 4

Dorothy Does Screenwriting

True courage is in facing danger when you are afraid.

"I am not much of a magician, as I said; but if you will come to me tomorrow morning, I will stuff your head with brains. I cannot tell you how to use them, however; you must find that out for yourself."

"Oh, thank you—thank you!" cried the Scarecrow. "I'll find a way to use them, never fear!"

"But how about my courage?" asked the Lion anxiously.

"You have plenty of courage, I am sure," answered Oz. "All you need is confidence in yourself. There is no living thing that is not afraid when it faces danger. The true courage is in facing danger when you are afraid, and that kind of courage you have in plenty."

—L. FRANK BAUM, *THE WONDERFUL WIZARD OF OZ*

From: "Oz" <ScriptProf@earthmail.com>
To: "Dorothy" <WannaBeScribe@netmail.net>
Subject: Your assignment

Dear Dorothy:
As requested, here is your assignment. Take your time with it and do it well.
Good luck, and don't make easy choices—make daring ones.

Wizardly yours,
You know who.

Writing Exercise #1

You only learn by doing, so please write three scenes and send them to me:

A. In the first scene, your main character arrives to meet someone and the environment feels strange, mysterious, awkward.

B. In the second scene, your main character re-enters this same environment (it could be the next day or ten years later). He or she is greeted by the same person from the first scene, but this time, the environment and the greeting feel warm, happy, positive.

C. In the third scene, as your main character re-enters this same environment, the person he or she is hoping to see is not there. The environment reflects a feeling of desolation, sadness, and alienation.

Don't use dialogue. Instead, use visual imagery and action (the basis of the filmic lexicon) to dictate mood and story. Create a compelling narrative, most of which takes place offstage and must be deduced from what is given in the three distinct, disparate scenes.

D. Also write a one-page character biography of the protagonist that includes aspects of backstory, physical characteristics, and personality traits. Once you write this, see how many of these aspects you can incorporate into the story in subtle and artful ways.

From: "Dorothy" <WannaBeScribe@netmail.net>
To: "Oz" <OzProf@earthmail.com>
Subject: So, whatcha think?

Dear Cardinal:

Attached please find writing exercise numero uno. I hope you get a kick out of it. Feel free to trash it accordingly. In addition, can you be more specific about the significant story turning points that I should be conscious of when I'm writing a script that corresponds to Hollywood standards?

I remain your ever faithful and humble servant,
Hard at Work in Kansas

P.S. Okay, I know we made a pact not to discuss your personal life, but how about mine? Don't you want to get to know me better?

Writing Exercise #1 Response

A.

FADE IN:

INT. LABORATORY—NIGHT

The room stands dark, silent . . .

Suddenly, the symmetrical rows of fluorescent lights flash
to life like stale lightning. Each flicker gives a brief
glimpse of the laboratory. The walls are a bright white,
clean, unused. At intervals stand stainless steel plat-
ing, signifying the entrance to a walk-in freezer or cab-
inet holding a myriad of medical supplies and scientific
instruments.

A countertop that encircles the entire room is forged of
the same cold steel. Rows of beakers and graduated cylin-
ders line the walls like glass soldiers.

The flickering stops, as dull fluorescent light fills the
room in an anesthetized bath, highlighting a large table in
the middle of the laboratory.

Roughly three feet off the floor, held by a huge steel
column at its center, the slick metal table resembles an
autopsy counter, only at each end are placed several steel
shackles. The room is cold, sterile, and empty.

A MAN, early 30s, stands at the door. Wire-rimmed glasses
encircle his dark eyes, which dart around the room. The
black frames of his glasses serve as a stark contrast to
his red hair, the color of cooling molten rock, which high-
lights his granite features.

His young eyes slowly pan the room until they focus on the
center table.

Walking forward, he runs his finely manicured hand across
the cold gray surface. He presses down lightly, as if test-
ing its strength.

Kneeling, he presses the side of his face against the
steel, looking across the smooth surface.

Rising to his feet, he walks and sits down at a nearby
steel alloy desk. The desk stands bare, except for a note
that reads "Welcome, Dr. Grader. Good luck."

The doctor now sits silently at the desk. He simply stares. We sense his troubling thoughts.

Finally, he stands again, and slowly makes his way to a huge metal door at the rear of the room. A complicated series of locks and latches line the perimeter of the massive door; they all click open in unison as he presses a sequence of numbers on a digital keypad.

The door opens, allowing a sea of liquid nitrogen vapor to escape onto the floor, encircling the doctor's face and body in a ghostly mist.

Cool green lights within the massive freezer paint a lime shimmer across his glass lenses.

INSIDE OF THE FREEZER—

We see a large glass cylinder, roughly two feet in diameter and four feet tall. Liquid nitrogen bubbles and percolates inside the glass, cooling the brain and spinal cord that reside within.

Dr. Grader offers a cunning smile as the lights flicker and MUSIC RISES . . .

FADE TO BLACK.

B.

FADE IN:

INT. LABORATORY—NIGHT—MANY YEARS LATER

The laboratory stands in disarray. Various diagrams and mathematical equations hang from every wall, covering the cold steel in a collage of ink and paper.

Plastic champagne glasses and an assortment of bottles are scattered throughout the room, as are paper hats, streamers, and other signs of celebration.

The door opens, and the fluorescent lights instantly spring to life as Dr. Grader stumbles in, an empty bottle of Jack Daniels clutched in his paw.

His brilliant red hair has dulled to a crimson rust, with streaks of gray. His eyes move like a child's at Christmas, while the rest of him slowly staggers across the room toward his desk.

Dr. Grader brushes an assortment of trash from his chair and collapses into it, the liquor acting as though it added fifty pounds to his weight.

Opening one of the many drawers, the doctor removes a stack of texts and notebooks, tossing them around the cluttered room as if he has no more use for them.

CLOSE UP—At the bottom of the drawer lies the faded WELCOME note, now grown sickly yellow.

Dr. Grader holds the note up to his face attempting to focus his drunken eyes upon the words. He finally recognizes it, and laughs hysterically.

Taking the note in one hand, he crumples it into a small ball, throws it amidst the other debris around the room and takes another swig from his bottle.

Smiling, he attempts to stand up again, fails, and finally manages to stagger over to the main table.

ON THE STEEL TABLE—

Is the striking figure of a young MAN. He is over six feet
tall, his pale skin pulled taut over a muscular frame. Long
needles protrude from his arms and legs, leading back up
into a complex series of chemicals and electrodes above
the table. The red hair and features of the man slightly
resemble the doctor, though certain parts have been . . .
exaggerated.

With a gleeful, childlike giggle, Dr. Grader kneels next to
his creation, brushing his fingers through the man's red
hair. He looks upon the silent figure as he would upon his
son.

In the freezer in the background, the glass cylinder stands
empty . . .

                    FADE TO BLACK.

C.

FADE IN:

INT. LABORATORY—DAY—A FEW WEEKS LATER

The scattered bottles and spilled champagne have now been replaced with blood. The once uniform fluorescent lights dangle from their sockets, swinging silently like glowing pendulums.

The doctor, a massive, still-fresh scar across the right side of his face, partially hidden beneath an eye patch, wearily walks across the room.

An occasional silent explosion of sparks showers the laboratory, highlighting the dented steel doors and frayed, exposed electrical wiring.

Slowly, and with a somber mask, the doctor walks to the center table. His hands run over the steel shackles, now reduced to twisted scrap metal.

A small puddle of dried blood paints a sickening picture across the steel platform, as the doctor runs his hand over his scar, remembering the massacre.

Taking his glasses off, placing them on his overturned desk, the doctor walks to a far corner of the room.

On the distant counter lay two severed arms, at their stumps extend a massive series of digital wires and titanium skeleton. The hands are covered in the dull crimson of dried blood, as a row of black bullet holes line the forearms and biceps.

Unable to bear looking at the severed limbs, Grader grabs them and throws them across the floor, causing another flash of sparks to fall to the ground.

Making his way around the hanging fluorescent lights and scattered debris, the doctor approaches the large freezer.

The door is now dented, the locks hang broken and worthless, as a flow of liquid nitrogen mist streams freely from the cracked steel.

Yielding to creaking hinges and the dull roar of steel
against steel, Grader opens the door to reveal the glass
cylinder.

INSIDE THE FREEZER—

The doctor stares at the contents of the glass cylinder:
the same brain and spinal cord as before. Only now, a section of the right hemisphere of the brain is missing, the
serrated edges scarred with black powder burns and riddled
with bullets.

The sad eyes of the doctor look at the motionless organ.
Grader inhales and then exhales loudly.

BACK TO THE LAB—

Closing the door, the doctor turns around and begins the
long walk to the exit.

In the dark cylinder, the spinal cord twitches with a small
spasm, its base brushing up against the glass.

Hearing the slight noise, Dr. Grader stops, and turns
around. He scurries back toward the freezer, lifts up the
cylinder, embraces it passionately and holds his dying
child in his arms . . .

FADE TO WHITE.

THE END?

CHARACTER BIO OF DR. ALEXANDER GRADER

Raised during the height of the "free love" movement in the late 1960s, Dr. Alexander Grader had always believed in serving the public good. However, Dr. Grader's view of the public good often differed vastly from popular consensus. A genius medical student at the University of California, Berkeley, Dr. Grader failed to graduate when he was expelled for punching the head professor in the face, following an argument about genetic manipulation. Unable to obtain a job at any hospital because of this incident, Dr. Grader plunged into depression and despair, while his skills died away in a flood of cheap alcohol.

At the bottom of his life, and only a few years out of medical school, Dr. Grader met the chairman of a high-tech commercial research company in the Bay Area through a bizarre accident. Saving the chairman from being killed by a runaway trolley, Dr. Grader was offered a debt of thanks and a warm meal. However, the chairman soon realized that his life wasn't saved by some bum but by a medical and scientific genius. Immediately offering his savior a job, the chairman gave Dr. Grader a position in the company doing genetic and cloning research, and experiments dedicated to preserving and prolonging human life.

Though raised in a moral family and taught the virtues of freedom and love in college, Dr. Grader has always been a highly competitive and steadfast man. Once setting his mind on a goal, Dr. Grader never strays from it or allows anything to get in his way. Though this is an admirable quality, it is also a personal shortcoming, as Dr. Grader never has had the time to find a wife or raise a family. The fleeting relationships he did have revolved around purely sexual needs, as he was always dedicated to his first and only love—hard science.

A powerful man, resembling someone who would be more at home in the Alaskan tundra than in a research lab, Dr. Grader often uses his obvious strength to "influence" the opinions of coworkers who might not agree with his point of view . . .

From: "Oz" <OzProf@earthmail.com>
To: "Dorothy" <WannaBeScribe@netmail.net>
Subject: Concretizing the abstract

Dearest Citizen of Kansas:

I'm sure you've lived a truly scintillating life that you find eternally captivating, but, to be blunt, I don't care to get to know you through anything other than your work. So, let's get to it.

Very well done. I'm glad to see it. Keep writing. Now, on to our next lesson.

The single most important concept that I want to convey to you during this, our second big lesson, is what I have come to call "Concretizing the Abstract." This is a term I believe I am the first to utilize, especially considering the fact that I coined it. What exactly does "concretizing the abstract" mean? Well, for me to answer that question, let us start at the beginning.

Try to pay attention.

Go in good health, kiddo,
Ozzie

Capturing Your Characters' Inner Lives

Since film is a visual medium, the screenwriter does not have the luxury of the novelist, who can convey psychological states through interior monologues, detailed thoughts, and omniscient narrators.

The only film technique that comes close to these novelistic devices is the voice-over, which tends to be overused, can be distracting to the viewer, and many times is utilized in a lame attempt to compensate for a poorly told story. As in, let's try to save *Blade Runner* by forcing Harrison Ford to do some voice-overs. Sure, it makes the film a little less murky, but in the end, it's more annoying than helpful.

Yes, there are times when voice-overs add to the filmic texture, but these are few and far between. In general, you should avoid them and instead develop your visual storytelling skills; in other words, you should learn to *concretize the abstract*. In so doing, you'll physically embody your characters' abstract emotional states of mind in concrete manifestations such as symbolic props, actions, and objects.

 THE CARDINAL RULE OF OZ

Always remember the cardinal rule of screenwriting workshops across this fair land: SHOW me, don't TELL me!

With this in mind, you will be able to avoid relying on weak, on-the-nose dialogue that lamely presents emotional states, such as "Wow! I'm so depressed!" or "Oh boy, I feel so happy!" Try to use what T.S. Eliot termed an *objective correlative*—an object that correlates to an emotion.

So then, when you are writing for the screen, think of scenes in terms of images, not words. Don't rely on dialogue for plot; let the images do that.

You see, by merely listening to the dialogue uttered by the actors on the silver screen, we can't know what's really going on inside the characters' minds, especially if they aren't talented performers. Therefore, it's your obligation as the writer to externally convey the complex interior states of your characters. It is your number-one priority as someone who writes for moving pictures to *concretize the abstract*: to externalize emotions, to find actions and objects that can embody inner emotional states.

Your Goal: Capture the Audience *in* Your Film

You want your audience to enter what Joseph Campbell, American writer and mythologist, called a state of aesthetic arrest—a temporary state of being in which one loses all sense of time and place and becomes lost in the world of the text; where there is no distinction between the screen and the seats, the actors and the audience, I and thou; there is only the shared moment of wonder. The audience surrenders all rational thought and allows the power of the moment to overwhelm them, to transport them from their aching joints, complaining spouses, financial problems, and drop them into the magical world of the story.

Think of it as a reverse of *The Purple Rose of Cairo*, where instead of the main character stepping out into the audience, each member of the audience steps into the main character's role on the screen. Or think of it in terms of James Cameron's *Avatar*, where the main character of that film has an avatar in that story but is also the avatar for every member of the audience watching the film.

Let me provide you with an example of this phenomenon. You are sitting in the movie theater watching one of those horrendous horror films such as *Saw*. It's a dark, scary moment in the film when a hot young teenager is being tortured . . . again. And, well, for fun, your ever-playful significant other sitting next to you forms her hand into a claw, shrieks, and scrapes the side of your neck. Your reflexes kick in and you do the only sane thing: you scream like a banshee, toss all your popcorn and Jujubes into the air, pelting your neighbors, and then, red-faced with humiliation and fear, you spend the rest of the film hiding under your seat.

Falling Out of the Sky into Your Film

Just as Dorothy falls out of the sky into Munchkin Land, you want the audience to fall into *your* world. Thus, the question for you is, how do I begin? Where do I start? What's the best way to go about writing my screenplay? Here's a simple four-step plan to get you started.

STEP 1: DESIGN YOUR MOVIE POSTER

A good place to begin: Imagine what the one-sheet (the poster) might look like for your film. What one image would go on the poster? What headline might be written across the ad for your picture in the Sunday paper? Just one line. That is all . . . for now.

Don't be afraid to be reductive. Yes, we live in a highly complex world, but the minds of most Americans, especially those who work in the entertainment industry, are amazingly Forrest Gump–like. So, force yourself to have clarity. Simplicity is a virtue. Master the ten-second story pitch. What is the concept or premise of your film? What's the hook? Can you sell it in one line? For example, the way you would describe *District 9* is, simply, *Alien* meets *The Fugitive* in South Africa.

This emphasis on simplicity will ensure that your picture is a so-called high-concept (usually big-budget, star-driven, premise-oriented) movie, which many in the industry believe is the most commercially viable kind. Maybe the simplest way to define high-concept is to explain what it's not. Think of high-concept pieces as not the more artistic, theatrical, so-called soft, low-concept, character-driven pieces that, even though they may be very well-written, are not as easily sold. And even if they are sold, the reason for the sale usually lies not in the script's concept but in the execution.

STEP 2: IDENTIFY YOUR THEME

Next, as you begin imagining your screenplay, ask yourself: What is the reason you want—YOU NEED—to write this story? In one or two lines, give the theme (this work is thematically about how love conquers all, crime doesn't pay, etc.).

STEP 3: BRIEFLY DESCRIBE YOUR STORY

Now, explain your story in a three- or four-line paragraph. Only include the basics here.

STEP 4: EXPLAIN YOUR STORY IN THREE ACTS

In three paragraphs (representing the three acts—beginning, middle, and end), tell the whole story.

That is enough . . . for now.

The Legitimate Art of Manipulation

Once you start writing your pages, don't show off. Readers know very quickly when they are in the hands of a master, a person comfortable in his or her own writing self. If you're good, you don't come off as attempting to prove how clever you are; instead, you come off as if you are *in control*!

Yes, control. This is a key word, and it is ultimately hinged upon another key word: trust. Trust the power of your writing to subtly convey all the necessary information to your audience; trust your words. If the reader doesn't get everything, that's okay. He might still get it on an unconscious level . . . or even if he doesn't get it on that level, that's okay, maybe he'll get it next time around, and if he still doesn't get it, maybe it's time for a new reader who hasn't been lobotomized, or maybe, just maybe, it's your fault. (Yes, I'm sorry to say it, but there is always the possibility that you can be too subtle. There is always the chance that you may have written something that is imperfect and you need to do another revision. Sorry, folks, but writing is rewriting, although that's another lesson entirely.)

WORK BACKWARD

Simply put, in every scene, every beat, every moment, know what you want your characters to do, and why. When a friend of mine was pitching his story to Steven Spielberg, the great director kept asking him, "What does the audience feel right now in the story?"

This is so important. You have to know what you want your audience to feel during every moment of your story, and then you have to legitimately manipulate those feelings to achieve your storytelling goals.

However, don't forget the contract you have with your audience: never tip your hand, never let the audience see what you are trying to do. If they feel as if they are being lectured to or manipulated, they will instantly reject whatever is being said, no matter how valid it might be. Since film is a visceral medium, if you appeal to your audience intellectually, you won't really have them until you've hooked them in the gut or grabbed them by the heart.

TRUST THE AUDIENCE

In the end, your work must stand on its own. Although it might be nice to attend every screening of your work, standing next to the screen with a long pointer, explaining all the symbolic imagery, you must trust that your work speaks for itself (especially if your movie appears on thousands of screens nationwide).

This issue of trust is a huge one for many writers, especially those who are aspiring. Most writers in film school either over-write their screenplays because they don't trust their readers or underwrite, planting their screenplays with so many obscure elements that there is no way in hell a reader will be able to pick up on any of them. Personally, it was not until after I graduated from film school and started writing plays for the theater that I understood this concept of trust. It was only after working hand in hand with actors and directors, day in and day out, polishing, revising, and listening to my work being performed in front of live people, that I finally started to intuitively sense the audience's needs and began to trust that my writing could fulfill them in a simple, straightforward manner.

As film is an invisible medium (the edits should be seamless to give the appearance of a flowing vision), so should your writing be seemingly organic, natural, without artifice. Audiences should believe that the actors are literally making it up as they go along. The dramatic arts are highly artificial, but done in such a way that they give the illusion of being without artifice.

From: "Oz" <OzProf@earthmail.com>
To: "Dorothy" <WannaBeScribe@netmail.net>
Subject: Our Next Exercise

Hey Dot:
Okay, as promised, here is your next exercise . . .
Go for it,
Oz

Writing Exercise #2

Your second assignment is to find an objective correlative in modern stage drama and/or recent films. Then explain how the author concretizes the abstract.

From: "Dorothy" <WannaBeScribe@netmail.net>
To: "Oz" <OzProf@earthmail.com>
Subject: Objective Correlative

Dear Ozzie:
Before I start this exercise, I must say, I'm still kind of sad that you don't want to know more about me personally, but for now I will respect your wishes and allow you to get to know me exclusively through my work. Although I must say, I hope that one day we can talk about more than writing.

Okay, in terms of your assignment, my answer is this: In Tennessee Williams's classic stage play *The Glass Menagerie*, the objective correlative is the glass unicorn whose horn gets broken in the second act by the gentleman caller.

Yes, a fragile sensitive little glass unicorn figurine. Fanciful? Beautiful? Tragic? Poignant? Phallic? Call it what you will, but baby, it brings with it a host of emotions. When it happens on stage, frankly, it's damn powerful. (And I thought you should know, I was the stage manager in our community theater production.)

Or what about in the Oz story? All the gifts that the Wizard gives at the end are objective correlatives, yes? I mean, the diploma given to the Scarecrow is just a piece of paper, since he has already shown intelligence in his actions. The Medal of Valor given to the Lion is merely an object signifying the courage he has shown in protecting Dorothy. The heart given to the Tin Man is again symbolic of the heart that the Tin Man has demonstrated throughout the story.

Or, in terms of modern films, how about the spinning top in the film *Inception*? On one level, the top is merely a child's toy, but over the course of the film, it is endowed with great meaning and significance.

Pretty good, huh? I bet you don't find students like me every day, now, do you?

Your single favorite student of all time,
Dying for more

P.S. Oh my god! Your lessons rock and roll! Don't ever stop, especially with the easy homework assignments. Do I have an A so far, or what?

CHAPTER 5

Structure, Theme, and the Broomstick Engine

Bring me proof that the Wicked Witch is dead.

"I am Oz, the Great and Terrible. Who are you, and why do you seek me?"

And the Lion answered, "I am a Cowardly Lion, afraid of everything. I come to you to beg that you give me courage, so that in reality I may become the King of Beasts, as men call me."

"Why should I give you courage?" demanded Oz.

"Because of all Wizards you are the greatest, and alone have power to grant my request," answered the Lion.

The Ball of Fire burned fiercely for a time and the voice said, "Bring me proof that the Wicked Witch is dead, and that moment, I will give you courage. But so long as the Witch lives, you must remain a coward."

—L. FRANK BAUM, *THE WONDERFUL WIZARD OF OZ*

From: "Oz" <OzProf@earthmail.com>
To: "Dorothy" <WannaBeScribe@netmail.net>
Subject: A structural lesson

Dear Cocky One:
I think it's closer to an A-minus and slipping into the B range even as we speak. And be careful, you're going to strain your arm and bruise your back if you keep patting yourself so forcefully. Hence, my friend, don't turn into a prima donna on me just yet, especially considering how far we still have to go.

Life, Only Better

The three most important concepts that I want to convey to you next are structure, theme, and the broomstick engine. Live by big Al Hitchcock's words, and imagine your story with the boring parts cut out.

Film and theater are reality, only better; they are heightened, hyperreal. Life zips by like a Blu-ray DVD on super-fast-forward, but once in a while, there are moments that move in slow motion and remain stuck in our memories forever. They are there for a purpose. They have an inherent power. Explore these moments. Why are they unforgettable? Pick the most dramatic events of your story and build your script around them. Don't be afraid to twist them around, to bend and shape them into art, so that they are always fresh and full of surprises.

Start with reality and then go from there toward narrative art.

"Drama is life with the boring bits cut out."

—ALFRED HITCHCOCK

It's the Story, Dorothy

As I mentioned earlier, you need to have a clear understanding of what story it is you are trying to tell. To do this, you should be able to articulate the answer to these two questions:

1. What is your *story* about?
2. What is your story *about*?

I know, I know—at first glance, these two questions appear to be similar, but in fact, they are worlds apart. The first question is one of plot. What is the A-level plotline? What is the dramatic problem or device that drives the film forward?

Now, the second question, which looks deceptively like the first, is simply, what's your story *about*—you know, thematically?

What are you trying to say? Your theme equals those elements in the film that are going to alter the way the audience thinks of the

 # THE BLIND SIDE OF TRUST

The film *The Blind Side* deals with the theme of trust—can and should people of different skin color and socioeconomic classes trust each other? The climax of this film is also the opening scene where the main character, Big Mike, is being grilled by an NCAA official, who forces him to question the motives of the family that took him, a family that he trusted. The film then flashes back to two years earlier and we see everything that he had gone through until we get back to the moment from the opening scene. And then, finally at the end of the film, the main character learns to truly trust and in doing so achieves greatness.

world after they leave the theater. This is where you are invited to be a little bit preachy, to have a point of view, to attempt to say something that can and should change the world. But tread carefully. If your theme is too obviously stated, or if it crosses the boundaries of what audiences feel is acceptable, or if it presumes to take the place of a plot, you're in trouble. You see, the theme holds together the bones of the story. Yet, it must exist as a subtext, as the roots to the story's blossom. The theme resonates throughout the story.

All well-crafted stories hinge upon at least one major dramatic question that is established when the inciting incident takes place. Will Harry and Sally ever be able to get together as more than friends? That film's theme is inherent in this question. The stakes change, the characters face more jeopardy, they make bigger and bigger choices, and a story unfolds. In the end, if we look closely, we can see that this wonderful story was really a huge lie told to illustrate a simple truth: Love can triumph over all.

Where's Your Broomstick Engine?

All stories need a plot device that drives the story forward, what I like to call a "broomstick engine." And, as you may have already guessed, this phrase comes from the point in *The Wizard of Oz* where the Wizard sends Dorothy, the Cowardly Lion, the Scarecrow, and the Tin Man on a mission. If they want the Wizard to grant them their wishes (respectively, home, courage, a brain, and a heart), they must do something for him: they must bring him the broomstick of the Wicked Witch of the West.

The broomstick serves as an engine, a powerful motivating device, what Hitchcock called a "MacGuffin" driving the story forward. (Think of "Rosebud" in *Citizen Kane*.) It is a device, it drives the story forward, but in the context of the story, it must not feel like a device. Good stories never feel artificial. In *The Wizard of Oz,*

REAL OZ VERSUS REEL OZ

In the novel *The Wonderful Wizard of Oz*, the Wizard actually only says, "Kill the Wicked Witch of the West" or "Bring me proof that the Wicked Witch is dead." This demonstrates the difference between film writing and novel writing. Novels are more psychological, while screenplays need to be more visual. Thus, in the novel, the author can be less specific and merely give the reader the general statement, "Kill the Wicked Witch." While in a screenplay—a visual medium—you are always best served by having concrete images driving the story forward—by concretizing the abstract. And so, in the script, the text has been altered so that the Wizard asks for a concrete, tangible object that represents the proof that the Wicked Witch is dead—hence the broomstick.

viewers must see the broomstick as essential for getting Dorothy home.

The magnificence of *The Wizard of Oz* is that in their efforts to capture the broomstick, Dorothy and her friends inadvertently develop the attributes they were searching for all along. In essence, in the process of achieving their immediate goal—the broomstick—they also achieve their long-term goals (a deeper understanding of home, of courage, of intelligence, and of love) that are then validated by the Wizard's speeches and his presentation of tokens, objective correlatives, representing each of these attributes.

The fact that the broomstick is merely a device to get them where they need to be emotionally, where they need to get to psychologically, is further proven by the ultimate status of the broomstick of the Wicked Witch. Dorothy and her friends almost die in their efforts to get the broomstick, but once they attain it, it is essentially forgotten. The broomstick is emblematic of where they need to be, and who they need to become. Once they grow and become their fully realized selves, the broomstick is no longer really necessary or seen as something of value.

Don't Forget about Danger and Desire

As inevitably as the yellow brick road leads Dorothy to Oz, the concept of the broomstick engine brings us to the concept of danger and desire. To be more specific: a *clear and present* danger and a *clear and present* desire/need.

Let's go back to Dorothy. In Act One, she wants to run away from home. (Please note, this is not in the book, but only in the movie.) In Act Two, Dorothy wants to go home, but that is not an easy thing to achieve. There are a great many obstacles in her path, but soon she determines that the best way to achieve her goal of getting home is to see the Wizard. Once she follows the yellow brick road and achieves this goal, we have come to the midpoint of the story and she needs a bigger, harder-to-achieve goal. Thus, the Wizard demands that now if she really, truly does want to get

 IT'S NOT ABOUT YOU

Screenwriting is never about the writer; it's always about the reader, the audience, the viewer. It's always about what turns them on, not what turns you on. As my father always used to say, "The bait must taste good to the fish, not the fisherman." Keep this in mind when developing your screenplay.

home, she must do the impossible: she must bring him the broomstick of the Wicked Witch of the West. And so the story works because it continues to escalate and the tension in the viewer never dissipates.

On the Edge . . . Again and Again

Constant danger leads to constant desire—and you need to constantly articulate this desire so the audience feels constant tension. This is the key—how the audience is feeling. The audience needs to care and the only way they can or will care is if you have made it clear what is at stake for the main character and why it is important that she achieve her goal. If the audience understands this and wants, really, really wants Dorothy to get home, then, and only then, will they keep watching and go anywhere you take them.

A Student's Tale of Danger and Desire

To further illustrate this important point, let me give you a specific example of an experience I had with a student at a screenwriting conference. Student X (as a sign of respect for the Hollywood Ten, I've never been one to name names) approached me with a story he'd been toying with for a long time but still wasn't happy with. The story told the tale of a college student who had to deal with the unexpected death of a parent. Student X was a bright kid who wanted to say a lot about the nature of a young person reconciling himself to the death of a beloved parent. So Student X had inner story, what some might call a strong B-level storyline, but essentially no A-level storyline. Student X needed a broomstick engine, if you will, to drive the thematic elements forward.

The more we talked, the more I realized Student X needed a funeral somewhere far away to serve as his broomstick. In other words, he couldn't just write about someone dealing with death, he needed to write a story about a young man who has twenty-four hours to drive 1,000 miles to get to his father's funeral (a physical embodiment of death). Over the course of his journey, this young male protagonist will be forced to reconcile and deal with the complex feelings that he has for his father that naturally occur when confronting the death of a loved one.

Once Student X agreed to turn his script into a road-trip picture, he still needed a strong antagonist, plot points, and complications to make the journey of his male protagonist to the funeral work as a mirror reflecting the inner journey his main character has to undergo as he learns to reconcile himself with death.

In the end, Student X learned that if you want to say something important, God bless you, but the world already has enough preachers. What the world needs now (besides love, sweet love) is more storytellers who thrill and entertain. After you've been enthralled by the wondrous tale of a master yarn-spinner, you might find that good storytelling also includes subtle messages that are covertly hung on the clothesline of a compelling story.

Beginnings and Endings

Movies evolved in the twentieth century into a commercial entertainment form in which formulaic dramas with conventional Aristotelian structure were mass-produced to deliver audiences into theater seats. Once seated, these moviegoers would be captive consumers of popcorn at exorbitant prices. The more popular the film, the more tickets sold; the more tickets sold, the more popcorn sold. And so, films that were popular with audiences = more popcorn = more money made. (Most people think what really counts are box office grosses, but at least for movie theater owners, it's all about the sales of popcorn and Goobers and Raisinets.) Thus, theater owners preferred popular films that tended to be different from but reassuringly similar to other popular films that audiences had already seen.

Hence, the rise of the Hollywood formulaic film. Viewers watched a story hinged upon a standard format in which a problem is introduced in the first act and solved by the third act—which closes, inevitably, with a happy ending (or a tragic one with hopeful overtones) that makes the viewers feel good about themselves and the world as they leave the theater. In the span of roughly 120 minutes, problems involving the protagonist (and in many cases, also a minor character in the "B" plot) are surmounted so that the protagonist may learn a valuable lesson and be united with family, spouse, loved one, and insignificant others.

These happy endings, marked by the loving union of family members, represent an affirmation of the human need to surmount death through displays of love, acts of redemption, and attempts at transcendence in the form of familial continuance (represented in many cases by marriage and/or children) and collective memory.

True, there has always been the classic American outlaw/anti-hero (think of Michael Corleone in *The Godfather*, Wolverine, Batman, or Tony Soprano in *The Sopranos*), who represents a darker American apocalyptic vision. Yet it is the Karate Kids, the Luke Skywalkers, and Indiana Joneses—the survivors who overcome death and tragedy—who are the truly archetypical American heroes.

THE ORIGINAL WIZARD: ARISTOTLE .

In order to discover more about the nature of beginnings and endings, let's go back and explore what is meant by traditional Aristotelian structure. In Gerald F. Else's 1967 translation of *Poetics*, Aristotle states that great drama is an imitation of an action that is complete and whole. More specifically, "Whole is that which has beginning, middle and end. '*Beginning*' is that which does not necessarily follow on something else, but after it something else naturally is or happens; *'end,'* the other way round, is that which naturally follows on something else, either necessarily or for the most part, but for nothing else after it . . ."

Thus, the average audience member, who is unconsciously attuned to this Aristotelian beginning, middle, and end model, will expect a certain structure (the *energeia);* if they don't get it, they will feel vaguely unsatisfied. In the first act of the story, all the necessary elements must be assiduously planted and twisted. Then, in the second act, these elements are turned around in unexpected ways. By the end of the third act, all these elements are paid off. In other words, the ending, the climax, serves as something, as Aristotle says in *Poetics,* that "naturally follows on something else, either necessarily or for the most part, but for nothing else after it . . . So, then, well-constructed plots should neither begin nor end at any chance point but follow the guidelines just laid down."

THE ENERGEIAC PLOT, ENDED

Another way to understand this theory of *energeiac* plots is summarized by John C. Gardner in his bible for modern writers, *The Art of Fiction.* In it, he states that endings should embody the "actualization of the potential that exists in the plot and characters." And so, when we find out who Keyser Soze really is at the end of *The Usual Suspects*, we cheer.

However, if a writer does not tie all his loose ends together or introduces elements that do not pay off or make sense within the context of the story, audiences have a strong negative visceral reaction to the story.

When the predominating *energeiac* structures that viewers desire are not present, audiences feel cheated, and, in turn, can get pissed off and end up hating the movie, or even worse, end up hating you for writing the despised film.

THE PROPOSAL
NO ONE BELIEVED

For an example of an *energeiac* structure that didn't work, take the Sandra Bullock romantic comedy, *The Proposal*. There was a lot that worked well in this film, but it lost me when Mr. Gilbertson (played by Denis O'Hare), the skeptical clerk at the immigration department, flies all the way to Alaska and then takes a boat to the remote island where the shotgun wedding of Sandra Bullock and Ryan Reynolds is taking place. Sure, the filmmakers realized this was a bit far-fetched, so they had a scene showing that Craig T. Nelson, Reynolds' father, supposedly flew the immigration officer there, but still, at that point, much of the audience had checked out and rejected the film. The main issue that this brings up is one of credibility. And if you lose credibility with your audience, then they will disconnect from the story.

Energeiac Structures and Comedies

In comedic films, these brittle seams show most clearly. For example, take basically any episode of *Family Guy*. The genius behind that show, Seth MacFarlane, was raised watching Hollywood TV and films. As a result of his deep appreciation and understanding of the rules of Hollywood storytelling, he finds tremendous humor in constantly exposing narrative implausibilities that exist in recent movies and TV shows and he does this to great comic effect. In fact, in every episode, there are a multitude of pop culture references to and parodies of TV commercials, songs, TV shows, and movies. Take, for example, the episode "Something, Something, Something, Dark Side," in which MacFarlane skewers *Star Wars Episode V: The Empire Strikes Back* and shows its story flaws and pretentions.

CHAPTER 6

Signposts Along Your Yellow Brick Road

You are in luck not to have a heart.

"Why, as for that," answered Oz, "I think you are wrong to want a heart. It makes most people unhappy. If you only knew it, you are in luck not to have a heart."

"That must be a matter of opinion," said the Tin Woodman. "For my part, I will bear all the unhappiness without a murmur, if you will give me the heart."

"Very well," answered Oz meekly. "Come to me tomorrow and you shall have a heart. I have played Wizard for so many years that I may as well continue the part a little longer."

—L. FRANK BAUM, *THE WONDERFUL WIZARD OF OZ*

From: "Oz" <OzProf@earthmail.com>
To: "Dorothy" <WannaBeScribe@netmail.net>
Subject: Not Kansas

Dearest Dot:
Okay, so now I'm back and the learning continues. Without further ado,
let me jump right back into it. And so, away we go . . .
Oz

You're Not in Kansas Anymore . . .

Dorothy, you are in Hollywoodland now, and in Hollywoodland,
there are a great many unspoken storytelling paradigms that must
be mastered. I have already mentioned some general ones in the
preceding pages. Beyond those, there are also certain page numbers
that typically correspond to significant story points. More on that
in a bit.

Please remember, these are not God-given formulaic points
set in stone that you must obey, but instead, only starting points,
guardrails, guideposts, foundation markers to help you navigate
the almost overwhelming superstructure of an entire full-length
feature. And note, these well-worn story points did not just appear
out of thin air. Here's where they came from:

1. These story points are the result of many bright people in
   Hollywood watching many award-winning films over the
   course of many years, and then these bright people started
   tabulating approximate times in which these story turning points occurred in all these fabulous films. These people then wrote memos and books and guides that became
   standard texts in the business and standard talking points in
   script development meetings.

2. Then, lots of very smart screenwriters in Hollywood read these memos and books and guides and received notes on their scripts based upon these story points and soon, as a result of their desire to get their scripts produced, they all started writing movies that incorporated these pre-established story turning points.

3. Thus, many movies with these pre-established story points were produced and distributed. Soon, millions of filmgoers watching these movies started to unconsciously expect all movies to follow this same story structure. In fact, audiences actually will now become disturbed and disappointed when confronted with a film that does not conform to this paradigm.

4. This self-perpetuating process continues today as screenwriters, development people, and audiences now expect movies to fit this paradigm with its standard story points.

And people wonder why so many Hollywood films seem formulaic!

 THINK LIKE PICASSO

These guidelines should provide support for the initial structuring of your story; however, there is always the possibility of them handcuffing you artistically. In order to avoid this problem, see these page markers as a sort of flexible boundary, an invisible fence. If they seem to be hamstringing you, instead of throwing your hands up in despair, try to be like Picasso. He mastered the academic tenets of light, shadow, and perspective at a young age and then spent the rest of his life deconstructing these rules and learning how to see and paint like a child again. Be childlike—but never childish and immature.

Page-by-Page Structure Breakdown

For what it's worth, here we go. I am using page numbers here based upon a standard 120 page—120 minute—script. Of course, if your script is only 103 pages, or 103 minutes, compress all these numbers accordingly. Remember, just because act breaks are not labeled or indicated in your script doesn't mean that they aren't there.

Act I

This section must be lean. No fat or extraneous details allowed.

- ✧ **pp. 1–10:** Setup. Establish theme and tone; expose the heart of your picture. What is it about?
- ✧ **pp. 11–25:** The story must be established. Your dramatic problem must be presented.
- ✧ **pp. 26–32:** Turn your story in a new direction. Reversal. Discovery. Twist. POW! Leading us quickly to the end of Act I: by page 32 your protagonist must experience a major turning point that sends us in another direction and changes her life forever. This turning point must relate to the A storyline. Also, the protagonist should confront the antagonist and fail; then, the fun really begins.

Act II

This act is the longest, and the most difficult one to write. This is also the only act where you can breathe, and explore characters and relationships.

✧ **pp. 33–45:** The B, C, D, or subplot storylines should have been established by now. These subplots deal with the main character's relationships, not the plot itself; for instance, the best friend, the parent, or the love interest who affects the A storyline but is not the driving force of the story.

Every ten minutes or every ten pages, you need action—Boom-Boom-Boom. Never let up. Always keep building, especially in action/adventure scripts. You always have to top yourself. In scene after scene, when the audience believes there is no way the main character can get closer to death and still escape, the writer must always find a plausible way out for the main character.

✧ **p. 60:** The midpoint. This is usually a high note that can only lead to a low note by the end of the second act. You can take a breather here, but it won't last for long.

✧ **p. 90:** The second act turning point—the major turning point for the protagonist, who should now be at her lowest possible moment . . . and THEN has a realization (the "ah-ha") that leads her to pick herself up by the bootstraps and rush headlong into the third act. This turning point affects the course of the rest of her life. It is a galvanizing moment— an essential plot point when the main character realizes something about herself or her world that she did not know before—and this epiphany changes her life forever. Our heroine finds the courage to confront something she has never confronted before.

ACT III

This act is a series of actions in which the loose ends are tied together, always building and rushing toward the climax and the end.

⬦ **p. 110:** Final jeopardy. Everything comes to a head. No more uncertainty. This point is usually a heightened experience for the main character and the audience alike.

⬦ **p. 115:** Epilogue. Now, get out fast.

⬦ **p. 120:** Fade out. THE END.

With these structural signposts in mind, try to create a scene-chart where you lay out the major scenes of the story on paper.

The Three-Act Structure, Goal by Goal

Although there are no clear act demarcations in a film except those that you intuitively sensed when watching the film, a trained eye will soon come to see that there really is something to this act-break thing; act divisions are not as invisible and difficult to discern as you might think. I like to imagine act breaks as similar to the Salvador Dali painting that initially resembles a bowl, and then when you look at it upside down, you realize it's a face, and then you can never see it as a bowl again.

Now that you are aware that a movie is structured in acts, let's examine the signposts of each act, goal by goal.

**"I do not paint a portrait
to look like the subject,
rather does the person grow
to look like his portrait."**

—SALVADOR DALI

Act I Signposts

1. Hook the reader with a dramatic problem.
2. Include your inciting incident.
3. Have a galvanizing moment that twists the story in a new direction, forever changing the life of the main character and launching us into . . .

Act II Signposts

1. Build your story. Take the stakes established in Act I and raise them even higher. You think it can't get any harder for our hero, but alas, 'tis possible. In addition, the conflicts grow more and more intense.
2. Reverse expectations, thus forcing your protagonist to take greater risks.
3. Make more and more interesting obstacles appear to prevent her from achieving her goals.
4. Avoid a linear series of scenes. Don't be too talky. Keep a sense of urgency and danger. Yes, the second act is where you can deepen your characters and have revelatory monologues in which they reveal the unplumbed depths of their gorgeous souls, but still, you gotta keep moving forward. Always keep moving forward with no fluff, no fat, only lean, muscular prose.
5. Does the dramatic problem now represent something larger than the protagonist's life? If your protagonist fails, so what? I gotta really care by now. Even though I've had a sixty-four-ounce Diet Pepsi and my bladder is on the verge of bursting, I have to be afraid to go the bathroom because I fear I'll miss something crucial. Keep your audience's swollen bladders glued to the seats and you've won.

6. The protagonist inevitably finds herself worse off at the end of the act than she was at the beginning. She must be at a crisis point. What the hell should she do now? The decision affects everything and always leads to . . .

ACT III SIGNPOSTS

1. This act needs to feel like a headlong rush to the finish. There is no room for fluff here.

2. Your climax has to be the biggest moment of your film. You should know your climax before you start writing and write backward. Like a maze, which is easier to navigate if you start at the end and go back to the beginning, the secret to screenwriting is that it's much easier if you know your ending before you start. Let me repeat, most writers need to know where they are going before they go there. Once the end is understood, the story merely becomes a filling in of beats that lead inevitably to this moment. And Lord knows, when you finally get to the climax, it's gotta be damn good!

3. You need a sense of resolution. Loose ends must be tied together. But the key is to tie them together in a way that was not initially anticipated. The audience is expecting the square knot, so instead, you give them a noose, and then watch 'em laugh and cry as you hang 'em with it. Even in romantic comedies where we know the lovers will get together and in tragedies where we know the hero will die, you must find an interesting, unexpected way for the lovers to get together and for the hero to die.

4. Remember, a clear resolution is the outcome of a positive crisis decision that empowers your protagonist to succeed in the climax. Your story must force your protagonist to make the decision that illustrates her character transformation and provides a stirring example of her emotional growth.

MIND YOUR SIGNPOSTS

Keep these signposts in mind as you work out your story, and you won't get lost on your way to the Emerald City.

The Basic Outline

Now that you have an idea of what each act should accomplish, it's time to think about the big scenes in your movie, the unforgettable ones, the ones that you are dying to write. Describe each of those big scenes in a few sentences and then put those sentences all onto the same page. Once they are all together, you have a basic outline. This basic outline is a good starting point for you to see the major beats of your story.

 # ADDING SURROUNDING SCENES

Once you look at your basic outline and get a clear picture of the major moments in your movie, the next step is to add the surrounding scenes that flesh out the story. In order to do this, traditionalists like to use notecards pinned to a corkboard, while many modern day whiz-kids enjoy using Post-it notes on their walls or even a Word document or a PowerPoint file, which can be set up to look like walls full of Post-its. Choose any method that allows you to plot out the course of your story and see the whole picture at once.

The Step Outline

One good way to organize all the major scenes in your script is with a master scene list or what I call a step outline. It should include at least fifty major scenes from your script—more than the Basic Outline. Here's how to create a Step Outline:

- ◇ List all your major scenes in order.
- ◇ Describe the scenes in a sentence or two. You need not include lines of dialogue, although if you think of a great line, feel free to jot it down now.
- ◇ Keep in mind that all the major scenes in your step outline should be essential to furthering the story. Each should have a *raison d'être*, and there should be some change in the status quo by the end of every scene.

And as you journey from scene to scene, think of alternating between high and low moments, happy and sad, interiors and exteriors.

 # SCREENWRITING IS LIKE SEX

Sex is fine for a few minutes, or, God forbid, a few hours; but imagine a daylong session of nonstop copulation, and what was once a pleasure soon becomes a miserable occupation. Yes, there is such a phenomenon as too much of a good thing. Remember that when you do your step outline. Make sure all scenes are furthering the plot in a meaningful and interesting way.

The Perfect Structure: *The Wizard of Oz*

Let me illustrate more specifically by taking you on a structural analysis of, what else, my favorite film, *The Wizard of Oz*. It's a truly classic example of the three-act Aristotelian structure in action. And gee, it works, it really works. This form intuitively appeals to us all, as we are so deeply indoctrinated in it from early childhood that we feel as if something is wrong if a script does not follow this structure. I watched this film on DVD and tried to capture it in step-outline form. Here goes—and feel free to play Pink Floyd's *The Dark Side of the Moon* as you read this:

MGM's *THE WIZARD OF OZ*—1939: A STRUCTURAL ANALYSIS

Directed by Victor Fleming.
Written by Noel Langley and Florence Ryerson
Based upon the book by L. Frank Baum

ACT I

1. Opening sequence. CREDITS OVER CLOUDS/WIND. An overture plays in the background. This film is dedicated to the young at heart.
2. COUNTRY ROAD—We start with tension. Dorothy Gale asks Toto, "Did she hurt you?" We feel the threat of the evil Miss Gulch. All in sepia tone.
3. FARM YARD—Aunt Em and Uncle Henry are too busy to be bothered now. Toto is in jeopardy from Elmira Gulch. (3 minutes)
4. ANIMAL PENS—We meet the shiftless farmhands. Hunk tells Dorothy to use her brains. Zeke talks of courage. Dorothy falls into the pigpen. Zeke saves her. He speaks a big game, but in reality, he is without courage—cowardly.

Hickory talks of erecting a statue to him. He will be known for his heart. Dorothy is imagining things. She needs a place where there isn't any trouble . . . She sings, "Somewhere over the rainbow." God's light shines down on her as she sings.

5. THE ROAD—(7:30 min.) Miss Elmira Gulch arrives in front yard. Toto bites her.

6. INSIDE THE HOUSE—Miss Gulch says that Toto is a menace and must be destroyed. Dorothy ought to be punished. Miss Gulch produces the Sheriff's order. Aunt Em says that they can't go against the law. Uncle Henry puts Toto in a basket. Dorothy calls Miss Gulch an old witch. Gulch runs half the county, but since Aunt Em is Christian, she can't say what she wants to say to her. (10 min.)

7. THE ROAD—Toto escapes out of the basket.

8. DOROTHY'S ROOM—Toto returns. Dorothy says to Toto, "We've got to get away." They run away.

9. THE ROAD—Dorothy and Toto run away. Meet Prof. Marvel.

10. PROF. MARVEL'S CAMP—(11:30) He tries to guess why she is there. He says, "You are running away . . . You want to see other lands." He reads her mind. Inside his trailer, they look at his crystal ball. He sees a photo—uses it to tell her future. In the ball, he sees her farm. He says that "Em is crying. Em is sick." Dorothy realizes she has to go home right away. She runs back home. A storm is blowing up. Marvel takes cover. He says, "Poor kid." A twister is coming.

11. THE FARM—(15 min.) The twister is coming. It's blowing hard at the farm. Aunt Em screams, "Dorothy?" Everyone takes cover. "Where is Dorothy?" They can't look for her now. They go into the storm cellar without Dorothy. Dorothy tries to get in. She can't. She goes to her room and gets hit by a window frame and falls onto the bed.

12. TWISTER MONTAGE—(17 min.) The house flies through the storm. Dorothy sees visions in the window. Miss Gulch turns into a witch. The house falls down and lands. Dorothy is safe. She walks through the house.

13. OVER THE RAINBOW—(19 min.) Dorothy walks into Munchkinland. It is beautiful, quiet. Empty. "Toto, we're not in Kansas anymore." Glinda, the Good Witch of the North, appears from a bubble. She says that a new witch has just dropped a house on the Wicked Witch of the East. So the Munchkins all want to know if Dorothy is a good or a bad witch. Glinda says "Only bad witches are ugly." So Dorothy must be a good witch. The Munchkins see her as their heroine, their savior from the Wicked Witch of the East. The Munchkins celebrate. We see their military, their horses. "Ding Dong, the Witch is dead." The Mayor declares a Day of Independence and says to Dorothy, "Welcome to Munchkinland." (29 minutes into the film.)

14. EXT. MUNCHKINLAND—The Wicked Witch of the West appears in a puff of red smoke. She asks, "Who killed my sister?" When she reaches to filch the ruby slippers off her sister's feet, they disappear and reappear on Dorothy's feet. The Witch is powerless in Munchkinland. The Witch says, "I'll get you, my pretty." Dorothy must get out of Oz to be safe. Which is the way back to Kansas? The Wizard of Oz in the Emerald City is the only person able to tell her the answer. Glinda warns her, "Never let those ruby slippers off your feet." Glinda also tells her to "Start at the beginning and follow the yellow brick road." Dorothy is scared. Glinda disappears. Dorothy chooses to follow the yellow brick road and she is off to see the Wizard. All the Munchkins say, "BYE."

END OF ACT I (33 MIN.)

Okay, you get the picture of how to do structural analysis now, right? So, I'm going to stop here and if you are so inclined, you can do this on your own . . .

What Is the Inciting Incident?

What, then, can you learn about story structure from this fine example? For starters, let's look at the important event that we call the *inciting incident*. What is the major piece of action, event, or incident that launches Dorothy on her journey? What occurs to upset the balance of this character's life? What forces her to make a compelling choice that will change her life forever? The inciting incident needs to immediately snag the reader or viewer by the throat, and when you, the screenwriter, have your audience in your clammy paws, by God, don't let 'em go. Sure, you gotta let them breathe a bit, but don't completely loosen your grasp until the story is resolved. Then, and only then, should you slowly, gently release them from your grip.

In the case of *The Wizard of Oz*, many people think the inciting incident is the twister, and in Baum's book this is true. But in the film, the inciting incident is actually when Dorothy runs away from her home. This inciting incident compels Dorothy to go on her journey, and as in all good stories, Dorothy's adventure is manifested as both an inner and an outer journey.

Dorothy's Inner and Outer Journeys

Let me explain. More specifically, in *The Wizard of Oz*, Dorothy travels down the yellow brick road in order to get back home. So, there is a memorable physical outer journey that she embarks on with her three friends. But along the way, she goes on an inner, emotional journey as well, as she grows, learns, and changes. Thus, along the way, she becomes less selfish and immature and more selfless and caring.

This inner and outer journey is not unique to *The Wizard of Oz*. In one of my other favorite films, *Stand by Me*, we come to see that the story is about more than finding a body. Sure, the initial impulse in the film is for the main characters to go find a dead body and become heroes. But over the course of the film, the boys start to redefine themselves and their idea of what a hero is. By the end, we see that their journey in search of a corpse is a really a journey toward maturity, adulthood, life, and masculinity.

Rising Action

This idea of a journey also leads us to a complementary concept of rising action in a story. Any good journey must be forward moving, but it also must move upwards, and the stakes and tension must always be increasing. Take *Stand by Me* again. In this film, our heroes are in serious jeopardy if they continue forward on their quest to find the corpse. The stakes are constantly being elevated. Their lives are constantly being threatened (by a train, leeches, monsters in the night, Kiefer Sutherland and his thugs) as they journey from one Near Death Experience (NDE) to another. It always seems as if there is no way the characters are going to get out of this situation, and the viewer doubts that the writer can ever top the previous scene. But, of course, as the story pushes forward, the heroes do escape, and the stakes, much to the wonderment and pleasure of the viewer, have been raised even higher by the writer. The scenes all get nearer and nearer to death, but still, our resourceful heroes find a way to elude the Grim Reaper.

This constant pressing forward is the literal definition of rising action in a story and the primary reason that most adventure stories end in physically high places. For example, in *Batman*, the caped crusader fights the Joker at the climax of the story and, of course, at the last possible moment, sends the poor Joker plunging to his death, a phallic impaling that constitutes a fitting and bloody denouement.

But Sometimes, Predictability Is Good

We always want more and more tension with less and less predictability, except in something like a romantic comedy, where we desire and need to see the ending we expect. Take *Sleepless in Seattle*, for example. In this film, we want, we need, to see the lovers come together at the top of the Empire State Building. This is no surprise. Yet, the film still works because the surprises in the film all revolve around not how the movie is going to end but, more importantly, how the lovers overcome seemingly insurmountable obstacles to get there. Or, in other words, the stakes must be elevated in such a way so that as the story progresses, the more we want the lovers to get to the Empire State Building and be together, the more it seems as if there is no way they ever will. We are constantly surprised by the sequence of events and as a result, enchanted by the story. And most importantly, we can't stop watching and caring!

No Way in Hell Dorothy Ever Gets Home

Another key screenwriting guideline is what I like to call "The No Way in Hell Factor," which must be present all the way up to the story's end. To see if it's present in your script, ask yourself, "Self, have I delayed the inevitable in such a fun, interesting, compelling way that even though it may be inevitable, at this moment, it appears impossible to achieve? Have I written it in such a way that the audience is constantly saying to themselves, 'With what has just happened to her, there's no way in hell the heroine will be able to achieve her goal in this story!'"

And yet, somehow, in some way, by the end of the story, the protagonist *does* achieve her goals and all is good in the world again. It's your job as a screenwriter to set up that doubt in the viewers, and then deliver on your promise to sort it all out in the end.

From: "Oz" <OzProf@earthmail.com>
To: "Dorothy" <WannaBeScribe@netmail.net>
Subject: Writing Exercise #3

Dearest Toto's Best Friend:
I hope you have fully digested everything and are now ready to show me how well you have mastered all the materials I have sent you. Here is your next assignment . . .

Yours truly,
Oz

Writing Exercise #3

Your homework involves doing a story analysis/step outline of an existing modern film that you can rent on DVD. Watch it three times. On your first viewing, watch it for pleasure. On the second viewing, list the major scenes and time them with your watch. On your third viewing, impose turning points and act breaks upon these plot points, then analyze specific aspects of the story in terms of how you believe they speak to us on a deeper thematic level.

From: "Dorothy" <WannaBeScribe@netmail.net>
To: "Oz" <OzProf@earthmail.com>
Subject: X-ray vision

Dear Art Structure, Writing Deity:
I hate you. I can no longer enjoy movies. I can no longer focus on the big screen; I'm always looking down at my watch, checking the time, and

disturbing my loved ones and anyone else in the vicinity. As the story progresses, it's as if I can see the skeleton underneath the skin. Now I know
how Superman must feel, always having X-ray vision and seeing Lois Lane's
skeleton instead of her sexy black thong and brassiere.

But enough, we must get back to the job at hand. Act breaks are funny
things. Before I met you, I felt them, but I was never really conscious of
them. Now I see them everywhere. Aargh!!!

Thanks a lot, bub!
Cross-eyed Scarecrow

P.S. I know we've agreed to establish a purely professional relationship,
you know, one of two minds meeting on a purely spiritual level, but I gotta
have something to work with here. I mean, even if you don't want to alter
the image I have of you from a photo taken years ago, how about some
family background? And more importantly, what are you writing these
days? You have this incredible body of work from the '40s until the early
'50s and then nothing until the '70s and then, once again by the late '80s,
nothing. What's up with that? Fine, you don't have to share a recent photo
with me, I can live with that. But I can't understand why someone like you
would ever stop writing. This I think you owe me. Please know that I am
asking you these things only out of love and respect.

P.P.S. After hearing you rave about it, I decided to do my step outline of *Stand by Me*. I learned a lot by doing it and so thank you for the
assignment.

P.P.P.S. How much longer are these lessons supposed to last before I
become a rich and famous screenwriter?

CHAPTER 7

Myth and the Mythology of Character

Pay no attention to the writer behind the curtain . . . or screen.

"*Y*ou must keep your promises to us!" exclaimed Dorothy.

The Lion thought it might be as well to frighten the Wizard, so he gave a large, loud roar, which was so fierce and dreadful that Toto jumped away from him in alarm and tipped over the screen that stood in a corner. As it fell with a crash they looked that way, and the next moment all of them were filled with wonder. For they saw, standing in just the spot the screen had hidden, a little old man, with a bald head and a wrinkled face, who seemed to be as much surprised as they were. The Tin Woodman, raising his axe, rushed toward the little man and cried out, "Who are you?"

"I am Oz, the Great and Terrible," said the little man, in a trembling voice, "but don't strike me—please don't—and I'll do anything you want me to do."

Our friends looked at him in surprise and dismay.

"I thought Oz was a great head," said Dorothy.

"And I thought Oz was a lovely lady," said the Scarecrow.

"And I thought Oz was a terrible beast," said the Tin Woodman.

"And I thought Oz was a Ball of Fire," exclaimed the Lion.

"No; you are all wrong," said the little man, meekly, "I have been making believe."

—L. FRANK BAUM, *THE WONDERFUL WIZARD OF OZ*

From: "Oz" <OzProf@earthmail.com>
To: "Dorothy" <WannaBeScribe@netmail.net>
Subject: A mythical journey

Dear Baffy Buck:

First of all, I still write, but I no longer write for public consumption. I write for myself, on yellow legal-sized pads. When these pads are filled, I date them, and throw them in a big cardboard box and never look at them again. This act of keeping a journal makes me happy and is the only type of writing I still enjoy.

Furthermore, if you really have so much love and respect for me, you'll understand that at a certain point in his life, the host can get awfully tired of all the parasites sucking the juice out of him. There's a plethora of vampires in this town who make a living by draining the *élan vital* out of creative types. After this went on for years, I finally said, "Screw it! Let the maggots find another host. I'm dehydrated, desiccated, and tired."

So I stopped producing new work and soon enough, voilà, they went away. Praise the Lord. Amen and hallelujah!

Now my life has become a simple, blessed thing. I live in a small rented house by the Pacific Ocean. I love the smell of the water and the sand. I have a mixed breed dog I rescued, Meshugeneh, who eats all my leftovers. I have an old Toyota Prius, Athena, that is paid for and fully insured. Every three thousand miles, we Jiffy Lube. The Souplantation offers make-your-own-salads (all you can eat, mind you) for $8.95. So, no more chopping veggies for this herbivore. There are several artsy-fartsy movie houses and a bunch of multiplexes all within ten minutes of here. I get in at the senior citizen rate and then sneak around and see two or three movies in an afternoon or evening. I will occasionally teach a seminar if asked. I do my own thing (I teach, I do not blow my own horn or tell war stories about the golden days when Sammy Goldwyn and I used to blah, blah, blah, yadda, yadda, yadda . . .).

Once in a while, a residual check appears in the mailbox and I buy a snack for my dog and treat myself to a frozen mochaccino, extra cinnamon (yum-o) after the Souplantation. And at the beginning and end of every day, I sit outside on my small porch and listen to the ebb and flow of the Pacific tide as I read.

Don't laugh. I love it. My whole life, I have always been playing catch-up ball. Stacks of newspapers, magazines, and books have cursed me. Always there, teasing, screaming, "Read me."

"NO, OVER HERE. READ ME!"

"ME FIRST! ME. ME. ME."

And now, thank God, the stacks have disappeared, I hope never to reappear. My *New Yorker* arrives on Thursday and I am finished with it by Friday, unless of course, it is the double fiction issue, which takes a good week. I have two hours every morning for the newspaper. I listen to books on CD in my car. I read novels at night and yes, no stacks, no catching up to do, no fear of someone referring to an article in the *New York Times* at a cocktail party and then, that awful sinking feeling of being out-of-the-know . . .

Yes, I am finally all caught up and well-read.

This I find to be the greatest miracle of my life. It's like every day is Sunday without the dread of an encroaching Monday. I can sit under my down comforter, Meshugeneh curled up against me, and lose myself in a great author's narrative. Ah, the good life . . .

Yours in Paradise,
The Happy Wizard

The Filmic Power of Myth

Your next lesson concerns myths and legends, and how they play a role in screenwriting. First, I'd like to argue that all hugely successful films, unconsciously or consciously, somehow tap into myths and legends that speak to the human condition. Yes, these films are successful for many reasons, but it seems to me that there is always at least one specific aspect of the story that uses myth to directly address some pressing topical issue that is going on in the culture.

Okay, let me backpedal a bit here. If hypercritical is your middle name, everybody on your block thinks of you as the local Roger Ebert, and you can dissect a film with the best of them, yet you still feel there's some deep psychological resonance missing from your work, what should you do? Turn to myths! In other words, learn how you can inject your storytelling with a powerful mythological serum.

Cultural Myths

First of all, the word "myth" has become a misnomer for something that is not true. For example, "Unicorns don't exist. They're a myth." This is unfortunate, since the most powerful myths tend to represent our truest, most deep-seated fantasies and desires. Myths, the collective dreams of a culture, use the narrative process to endow our individual perceptions of the world with meaning. Operating on both personal and cultural levels, they are an invisible force that constantly drives us. Think of them as a sea of ideologies in which we are always swimming. Understanding myths will help us explain our lives.

Storytellers have a responsibility to pay attention to the cultural myths and tales of their day. Cultural changes that used to take decades or centuries to evolve are now happening practically overnight. The world is in massive transition. The new myths of science, medicine, and politics are constantly in flux. Witness the new stories and myths and beliefs surrounding the issue of climate change. Witness the crumbling of Wall Street and the U.S. economy in the late 2000s and dissolution of the myth of free enterprise and capitalism. Witness the success of any bestselling book or incredibly popular film and try to understand what it has tapped into in our culture. Try to decipher what issue or issues in our constantly changing society this work of art has addressed that has led it to become so popular.

Explore Your Own Personal Myths

We are also ruled by myths on a more personal level. As a child, you are indoctrinated into believing in certain myths: Santa Claus, the Tooth Fairy, parental infallibility. As an adult, you need to become conscious of and explore your own personal mythologies. Why do you act the way you act, believe in certain things, or even behave a certain way? These are all invaluable questions that you should answer to grow as a screenwriter and a human being.

Think of it this way: During the course of our lives, we convince ourselves of the validity of a certain personal ethos that dominates the way we conduct ourselves. For example, Daddy always said I would never amount to anything, and I have spent my life proving him right. Many students tell me of a schoolteacher who once told them that they were not good writers; as a result, they have internalized this myth, and now it is a part of their own reality that they must overcome if they ever want to feel good about themselves as writers.

 # STEPHEN KING AS MYTHMAKER

Take a moment to consider our successful modern mythmakers. Stephen King is able to intuitively sense our fears and articulate them in the form of monsters—material embodiments of our deepest phobias. In doing so, he is making them concrete, real, visual, and perfect for film. And over the course of the story, we, as individuals and as a culture, are healed by watching the hero in the story triumph over his monsters, which, most importantly, are also representative of our own demons.

Your Myth Is Your Story

So, find your myth by telling your story. Tell it over and over again, always changing it based upon audience reaction. Find its rhythm. Which details have you winnowed out? Which details keep reappearing, winding themselves through your stories? These are the true and wonderful guideposts that let our lives transcend the mundane to become art. Your job is to put the story out there. As you tell your story and it resonates with your audience, it should develop organically. If you have intuitively allowed the story to grow and change, it will tap into your audience's collective psyche and affect them.

Joseph Campbell Lays It Out for You

More specifically, Joseph Campbell stated that myths can be divided into four categories:

1. Myths that relate to the origins of the world and the way the world works;
2. Myths of the human life cycle from birth to death;
3. Myths that explain our relationship to work and other humans; and
4. Myths that explain the great mysteries of the cosmos.

Based on these distinctions, we see that there are old cultural myths and also present-day cultural realities that inevitably clash with these myths.

As a result of this clash, Cultural Myths versus Cultural Realities, we have a gap that needs to be bridged.

For example, you have the worn-out cultural myths that are supposedly ruling our society, the ones that show us the way things are supposed to be. They teach us, for instance, that crime does not pay. This theme is demonstrated in most traditional Hollywood films, wherein the bad guys get either killed or imprisoned and punished by the end of the film. So these stories are telling us that wrongdoers always get punished. However, on the other side of the gap, we see the harsh cultural reality that, on a daily basis, bad people are getting away with murder. We see drug dealers living large. Thus, a slight discrepancy appears that needs to be reconciled and a new myth, a new kind of story, needs to be told that speaks to this situation.

Capture the Empty Spaces

Yes, you as a modern-day storyteller have the mission of bridging this gap with your stories. As the poet Pablo Neruda said, capture "the holes in the fishing net," and fill them with your poetry and art. Write the myths that inspire us to be better human beings, that answer the difficult questions of being alive, that help structure our existence and imbue it with meaning.

The Mythology of Three Popular Movies

To see how successful screenwriters bridged the gap between cultural reality and cultural myth, let's look at *Forrest Gump*, *Home Alone*, and *Avatar*. Each approaches the gap differently but still reconciles it in the end.

The Mythology of *Forrest Gump*

Let's look at a hugely successful film—*Forrest Gump*—and how it bridges the myth-reality gap. On one hand, you have the cultural myths, "If you listen to your mother, you will succeed. If you work hard, you will succeed. If you love blindly and monogamously, you will succeed." On the other hand, we all are confronted with the day-to-day reality that many good people who work hard, listen to their mothers, and love blindly do not succeed. And thus, a discrepancy appears.

Never fear, Forrest Gump is here to bridge this gap, to overcome this discrepancy. Forrest can rewrite our history and in doing so, heal us. Through his simple, innocent perspective, he shows us that we are all simple, good people. He single-handedly makes us feel better about ourselves. Think of him as yuppie Liquid Paper, low-IQ Wite-Out. After watching this film, we can see Vietnam, Watergate, and all the assassinations of the past thirty years through the eyes of an innocent, and in so doing, eradicate the complexity of our history. We can, in fact, rekindle our sense of American purity and grace. Forrest teaches us the simple lesson that we aren't such bad people; it was just a tough time. And as long as we work hard, listen to Mom, and love blindly, everything will, in the end, work out okay. Trust me. Trust Forrest and everything will be okay, as it is by the end of the film.

THE MYTHOLOGY OF *HOME ALONE*

You still aren't convinced? Okay, then, take the movie *Home Alone*. This film attempts to reconcile the myth that we can leave our children home alone while we work all day and they will be safe with the reality that children who are left home alone are kidnapped, raped, and killed. Thus, this simple comedy speaks to us all. It appeals to all our latchkey kids who have been left alone and feel insecure about taking care of themselves, and it also speaks to all the parents who have to leave their kids at home alone and worry about their safety. So we can all watch this film and feel less guilty. If I'm a child, I'm empowered; if I'm an adult, my fears are assuaged. Either way, this film makes us feel better about ourselves, and so we spend lotsa moola to see it over and over again and buy the DVD and all the accompanying merchandise.

If you don't believe this is true, just read Paula Munier's wonderful memoir, *Fixing Freddie,* in which she describe moving back to California with her son for a reconciliation with her ex-husband. When this does not work out, her son, Mikey, was so heartbroken that he watched *Home Alone* every day for six months. True story, baby!

Yes, good stories tap into our aspirations and also provide solace and can be empowering.

THE MYTHOLOGY OF *AVATAR*

Or take the recent megahit, *Avatar.* James Cameron has a keen mind, and that film, though it takes place in the future and in a faraway land, is, of course, speaking directly to our treatment of the environment and our alienation from nature. Think about it. Basically every big issue in the environmental/green movement is present—threatened rainforests and innocent native people; evil, foreign big-business interests and the green theme of the interconnectedness of all things in nature. Yet, Cameron's genius, beyond his amazing visual style, is his ability to tell a deeply human love story, or should I say, Na'vi-human love story, in which we don't consciously register the fact that all these eco talking points are being brought into the story. Instead, we get caught up in the adventures of the characters and our desire for the lovers to be together and to stop the bad guys from taking over their planet. Thus, the story and the theme work together in such a way that we can feel good about watching this movie as it speaks to our aspirations about solving our own environmental problems.

Over the years, there have been a lot of cool-looking movies and there have been a lot of environmentally themed movies, but *Avatar* is really the first film to unite these two core concepts together in such an appealing way. And maybe the single greatest form of proof of this fact is that the world has spent more than $2 billion on tickets for this little flick.

Write Your Favorite Myth

Another beauty of using myths is that you can never say that you don't have anything to write about. Our society is perpetually filled with questions, tensions, problems, topical issues (overpopulation, violence, crime, terrorism, global warming, injustice) that all need to be resolved so that we can live with ourselves and others. When you see injustice, it is your job to create the next *Avatar* or *Spiderman* to right the wrongs of an unjust world. When you see a lack of romantic love in our world, it is your job to create the next Miley/Mandy/Amy/Zooey vehicle to teach us how to love.

BRIDGE THE GAP TO GLIMPSE A BETTER WORLD

In bridging the gap, do we really right the wrongs of society? No, of course not. In most cases, we just enjoy losing ourselves in a newly mythologized cultural reality, if only for two hours. But I believe that by losing our sense of reality, if only for a short time, we get an opportunity to envision a better world and ourselves in a better light. And in the end, you can only hope that some greater good may come of these ephemeral glimpses.

The world needs to hear from you. Tell your tale, and your myth will transcend the individual to embody the fears, passions, and desires of the culture as a whole. If you learn to tell your own story, you will also tell the story of all people. And your audience will embrace you.

How to Create Characters with Depth

So now let's get to it. It's not enough to bridge the mythology gap for your audience simply with plot, you have to do it with characters your audience will love—and love to hate. How do you build three-dimensional characters that jump off the page and throttle you?

Very carefully.

THE SCABBING-THE-WOUND THEORY

Lucky for you, I have a theory on character construction. Trust me, this one might even be better than Concretizing the Abstract. I call it Oz's Theory of Scabbing the Wound. In simplest terms, it states that all main characters are wounded souls, and the stories we tell are merely an acting-out of the healing process. They are the closing of open wounds, the scabbing-over process.

One of my favorite examples of this is the film *(500) Days of Summer*. In this movie, the main character, Tom Hansen (played by Joseph Gordon-Levitt) believes that he is meant to fall in love and spend his life with Summer Finn (played by Zooey Deschanel). However, over the course of 500 days, we see that he has a tremendous amount of baggage, preconceptions, and wounds associated with romantic love and affairs of the heart. As the film progresses, Tom is forced to realize that he loves a woman who does not love him. He has to relinquish his love, and in conjunction with this, his preconceptions about romance. As a result, his wounded heart is finally scabbed over, and he is healed. In the final scene, we see proof of this healing as he meets another woman and only now is truly and fully able to love and be loved. Damn good stuff, if I do say so myself . . .

USE A CHARACTER ARC

Another way to think of this phenomenon is by considering the concept of the character arc, i.e., the movement, the transformation, of the character over the course of the story. Character arc is played out in most stories. Characters start in one place and arc over the course of the story toward another emotional place. For instance, in Charles Dickens's *A Christmas Carol*, Scrooge starts as the most selfish man in the world and over the course of the story (and one night) turns into the most selfless man in the world.

THE FREUDIAN SCREENWRITING SLIP

Yet another way to think of this concept is in Freudian terms. All characters act out of what Freud labeled as the separation and individuation drama. Before birth, we exist in a state of unity and serenity in which all our needs are met. Freud's belief was that once we leave the womb, the rest of our lives are a struggle to return to that gone but not forgotten state of complete security, wholeness, and closure. What I find so interesting about this hypothesis is that these three elements—security, wholeness, and closure— correspond exactly to the basic tenets necessary to achieve the classic Hollywood happy ending.

This being said, you and your characters will be judged not by whether you achieved closure, but by how you and your characters acted over the course of their struggles. We all face the question— how have we gone so far away from home, and how the hell are we gonna get back in one piece? (To wit, think about our dear little twelve-year-old, pony-tailed friend Dorothy Gale, once again.)

Growing the Peach Pit of an Epiphany

Inherent in who we are is all that has befallen us and all that is going to befall us, both good and bad.

When we first meet your main character, her climactic epiphany should already be a peach pit buried deep within her soul, and it is only

"Character is fate."

—HERODOTUS

PREDETERMINISM FOR DUMMIES, ER, SCREENWRITERS

For more information on this theory of human potential and pre-determinism, see James Hillman's brilliant book, *The Soul's Code*. In a nutshell, we care about characters who care deeply about something. It does not matter whether that something is mundane or extraordinary. In *The Wizard of Oz*, all Dorothy wants at first is to get away from home, and then when she gets her wish fulfilled via the twister, all she wants is to get back home. Or take another classic film example: In *Dog Day Afternoon*, the main character (played by Al Pacino) holds up a bank to get money for a sex change operation for his lover. Now, this might not be a good reason for you to hold up a bank, but for him, it is the best reason in the world.

through a series of events that she, if forced to struggle with her peach pit, is allowed to grow into the fully mature peach tree that has lain dormant within her since we first met her.

CONFLICT + CHANGE = EPIPHANY

This, then, is your job—figure out the answers to these questions: How do you keep your characters constantly in conflict as they journey toward closure? What are the obstacles and conflicts, both inside and outside your characters, that they must face along the way? What is the worst thing in the world that could happen to them and then, of course, does it happen? How much do your characters change in order to get what they want? Keep them uncomfortable and they will expose themselves, and by exposing ourselves and turning ourselves inside out, we grow.

Conflict breeds change.

And change is what the audience desires and needs most for a satisfying filmgoing experience.

Character Development, Act by Act

Introduce your main character early in order to set up your dramatic problem. Establish the character's full backstory in the second act. Find a moment when she can have a monologue that reveals the colors and sounds of her soul, her deepest dreams, fears, and secrets. Let her breathe and scream and stink.

By the third act, characters must be fully fleshed out because by now there is no room for personality surprises. When you get down to it, characterization is a fraud, and it is up to you to create *credible* frauds. And always, the key to believability is specific details. Be specific. Specific. Specific.

A Character's Goal Can Change

As you write your first draft, you may find that your main character has an initial goal that may turn out in the end to be a false goal. In many cases, it is only over the course of the whole story that the character's true goals are uncovered and achieved. For example, let's look once again at my all-time favorite. In *The Wizard of Oz*, at first the story seems to be about Dorothy Gale trying to escape her home, but of course it turns out that the movie is really about her trying to return home.

It's Not All About Dorothy

Don't forget about the antagonist! This is the character that drives your story and your protagonist forward. The antagonist must be real, natural, believable, yet sure to give the protagonist a run for his money. The antagonist must be seemingly more powerful than the protagonist. It is the protagonist who needs to be resourceful and find the means to overcome the antagonist. This is the dynamic give-and-take, the Felix and Oscar Odd Couple Syndrome, the yin and yang, the unity of opposites that Lajos Egris talks about in his classic book, *The Art of Dramatic Structure.*

LET YOUR CHARACTERS SURPRISE US

The final factor that makes characters three-dimensional is a certain contradictoryness or multisidedness; in other words, characters who aren't exactly what they appear to be. For example, in a wonderful episode of one of my great guilty pleasures, the TV series *Glee*, "evil" cheerleader coach Sue Sylvester (played by the great Jane Lynch) appears to be a selfish, tyrannical b*tch, as usual—but by the end of this episode, we see that she has a sister with Down syndrome whom she cares deeply about and visits often. This is an unexpected and powerful revelation that humanizes her character, and makes us see her in a completely new and different light.

From: "Oz" <OzProf@earthmail.com>
To: "Dorothy" <WannaBeScribe@netmail.net>
Subject: Surrender Dorothy

Dear Somewhere over the Rainbow:
Here is your next assignment. May it be an enlightening experience for you to partake in.

God Bless,
Ozzie

Writing Exercise #4

Describe a colorful, three-dimensional character from your past. Try my patented digital snapshot technique, whereby you pick specific moments from your life and visually frame them, fully describing them, coloring them in as if they are glossy digital photographs. Don't forget to employ details to make your character spring to life.

From: "Dorothy" <WannaBeScribe@netmail.net>
To: "Oz" <OzProf@earthmail.com>
Subject: Check out Writing Exercise #4

Dear Prof.:

Sometimes I feel that you must have known my father. I mean, just like you, he always used to talk about doing stuff to build my character. You know, if this situation would have come up before I met you (I realize we haven't ever really met, but you know what I mean), I would have told you to go fry ice. However, I think I'm really growing as a character, so I'll indulge you and not project any of my deep-seated psychological issues with paternal authority onto you.

As you might say, enough for one day. I hope this assignment was close to what you were looking for. And to be honest, even if it wasn't, I enjoyed writing it and learned a little something.

All my best and thanks for all your guidance,
The Sort of Dorothy Who Will Never Surrender

P.S. Attached please find some snapshots of my grandfather coupled with a bit of analysis and self-consciousness to properly frame them. I hope this is in accordance with what you expected.

Writing Exercise #4 Response

1. *I am eleven years old. It is six o'clock, Saturday morning. I am standing in my flannel pajamas in my grandfather's kitchen. White. Shiny white Formica with gold specks. Silver chrome. And appliances from the fifties. In his chair at the head of the table, he is eating a toasted corn muffin with cream cheese. Breakstone's Temp Tee whipped cream cheese. His white, creamy spread of choice. To my grandfather, the downfall of Western civilization, the decline of mankind, the state of the world could be measured by the price of Temp Tee. I'd hear him tell my mother, "Do you know how much they charge for Temp Tee at Stop &Shop? Ninety-five cents. Racketeers . . . Thirty-nine cents. I used to pay thirty-nine cents . . ."*

2. *After breakfast, we'd get into his Cadillac. This was back when the word Cadillac carried weight. It was the epitome of LUXURY. Yacht-like. Gargantuan. Gold-toned. With monster-sized tail fins. It smelled of twenty-dollar bills, Vicks cough drops, and wet leather gloves. But the best part about it was in the center of the back seat there was a thick, cushy armrest that you could pull out and sit on. If you were a kid, it was the best place in the whole car to sit. Better than five phone books piled high, it was a mighty powerful perch, but supple. Soft. Comfy. Shaped exactly right for a kid's butt. When I sat there, I felt gigantic, strong, important, like a big* macher *(Yiddish for bigshot). Sitting there gave me an appreciation for what it must feel like to be my grandfather.*

3. *When we got out of his car, he'd take my small hand in his callused palm and we'd walk down the main street of Terryville toward his huge office in the biggest furniture store in the whole world, The Terryville Furniture Store, which stretched across a vast portion of the downtown Terryville area. A series of white warehouse buildings, it spread out like an enormous cherry tree*

in full bloom. And as we walked, I'd always hear people whisper to each other, "That's Harry Simon! He owns The Terryville Furniture Store."

4. *On the way home, as the sun would set and its golden rays would pour in the side windows of the car, I'd sit on my plush throne and ask my grandfather to tell me a story about what his life was like when he was a small boy. "Tell me, Grandpa. What was it like?"*

He would clear his throat and tell me of when he was five years old. A poverty-stricken child in a cold shtetl (village) in eastern Europe. A boy wearing his only pair of woolen knickers, knees patched over and over again. The material chafes his inner thighs. The dirty rainwater seeps through the holes in his shoes and socks, freezing his feet. His white shirt is three sizes too big. The only warm, solid thing in the world is his little sister's hand, gripped tightly in his own. His parents are gone. Missing. No tears. He will not let himself cry, but he is scared. Cold. So cold.

He is in hiding. If he is discovered, he will be killed. He knows this. He tries not to breathe. To not make a sound. He is hiding under the rotting wooden floorboards of his front porch, crying, frightened, watching as Cossacks on horseback storm through his shtetl, brandishing silver swords, killing men and women, five-year-old boys, destroying homes, setting them on fire, raping, pillaging, engaging in awful, unthinkable deeds as he cowers and prays and a deep, unquenchable rage grows in him.

The rage gives him the strength to work hard and save money and go to America where he will not be persecuted for being a Jew. And so, this is not a snapshot of fear, but of emerging strength, for the Cossacks failed in their mission to destroy him. Instead, they drove him forward, instilling him with the discipline, the power, the force of character to survive and, even, to succeed!

CHAPTER 8

Dialogue, in Which Dorothy Speaks/Sings/Delivers a Revelatory Monologue

I am Oz, the Great and Terrible.
Who are you, and why do you seek me?

"**I** am Oz, the Great and Terrible," spoke the Beast, in a voice that was one great roar. "Who are you, and why do you seek me?"

"I am a Woodman, and made of tin. Therefore I have no heart, and cannot love. I pray you to give me a heart that I may be as other men are."

"Why should I do this?" demanded the Beast.

"Because I ask it, and you alone can grant my request," answered the Woodman.

Oz gave a low growl at this, but said, gruffly: "If you indeed desire a heart, you must earn it."

—L. FRANK BAUM, *THE WONDERFUL WIZARD OF OZ*

From: "Oz" <OzProf@earthmail.com>
To: "Dorothy" <WannaBeScribe@netmail.net>
Subject: Dialogue

Dear Chatchkala:

You're making me proud. I knew you had to be good for something. Now, let's move into the realm of dialogue. Succinctness is the key here.

What are characters without dialogue?

Silent.

And sometimes, silence is good. As a screenwriter, you must be a visual storyteller and learn how to tell stories with images. So, if you can write a scene that works visually, do it, but there are also times when characters need to say something. Thus, the need for dialogue eventually arises.

Precisely yours,

The Dialogue Wiz

Making It Look Easy

Since *The Jazz Singer*, the first feature-length film with synchronized dialogue, screen characters have been endowed with the gift of language; they can breathe, and swear and scream, but be forewarned: Joe Gillis was right.

> "Audiences don't know somebody sits down
> and writes a picture; they think the actors
> make it up as they go along."

—JOE GILLIS IN *SUNSET BOULEVARD*

Just as Joe (played by William Holden) said in *Sunset Boulevard*, in good movies audiences really do believe that the actors are making up their lines as the movie progresses.

And that's what audiences should think—when, of course, the dialogue is well-written. But mark my words—having characters appear as if they are speaking naturally is no easy feat. Still, if you understand that writing dialogue is really an exercise in verisimilitude, an application of powerfully deceptive smoke and mirrors trickery, you will be well on your way to achieving Joe Gillis's paradigm of writerly invisibility. And I refer to smoke because dialogue relies upon hazy misdirection and ambiguity; mirrors, because these smoky shafts of dialogue must be reflected back onto your main character.

The Wizard's Formula for Good Dialogue

Thus, in order to achieve the ultimate in modern smoke and mirror effects, the first rule is

Be concise.

If you have a choice between saying something in one word or in one sentence, always pick the word. Many times when I read students' scripts, I can eliminate about one-third of the dialogue. In doing so, the scenes become three times better.

THE WIZARD'S DIALOGUE THEOREM

$D - \frac{1}{3}D = 3D$

I know my theorem looks mathematically impossible, but writing ain't a science, it's an art, and in art, when we carry around our little laminated poetic license, we are allowed certain liberties. So, my friend, please keep it short. Keep it simple. And never forget the ancient Greek epigram of the great poet, Syphilis: *Brevity is the filet of soul.*

The Wizard's Artsy Rule of Dialogue

Artifice is our next key element. Here's the Artsy Rule:

Use artifice, but don't be artificial.

'Cause it don't mean a thing if you can't make it sing. Let me explain. If you were to leave a digital recorder on in a booth in a Starbucks Cafe where two people were eating and then transcribe the dialogue verbatim onto a page, it would not read like good dialogue, even though, yes, it was real (whatever that means). You must focus on the *appearance* of reality, or what is called writing with verisimilitude. Your job as a writer is not to write dialogue that is real; your job is to create dialogue that *sounds as though it is real*—and hopefully, a bit more clever than real life. The distinction here—the "sounds as though it is real" part of the equation—is everything.

Mastering Expository Dialogue

The problem that arises is that there is usually some vital expository information that, no matter how hard you've tried to convey it visually, ends up having to be spoon-fed to the audience through dialogue. Then, when your character articulates the necessary information, that destroys the flow of your script, weighing your story down with awkward, heavy-handed speech.

What is the answer? Well, here is a technique I have found that may help. When you need to include exposition in your dialogue, ensure that it does not sound false by inserting it in scenes rife with extraneous action, heavy with conflict, and subtle, off-the-nose references.

THINK AUSTIN POWERS

A great example of this phenomenon occurs in the comedy *Austin Powers: International Man of Mystery*. As in all spy dramas, there is a tremendous amount of expository information that must be given to the audience (usually administered by an audience surrogate in the film who asks lots of banal questions). The author and star of this comedy, Mike Myers, has the two main characters convey the essential mystery-solving info while he and Elizabeth Hurley are disagreeing. But since this is a comedy, he also has Hurley's character walking around naked, her private parts perfectly covered by Myers's synchronous movements as he does the most British of acts—makes tea. The screenwriter Myers is successful here because as the audience laughs hysterically, they are not aware that they are also being spoon-fed the expository information they need to follow the complicated plot.

Give Characters Their Own Distinctive Voices

Remember, each character must have a distinctive voice. In real life, people employ particular jargon and speech patterns that characterize their own perspective, backstory, past, and socioeconomic station. In the film *The Blind Side*, the poor African-American Big Mike character (played by Quinton Aaron) must never speak like or use phrases that are similar to the language used by the wealthy, white Leigh Anne Tuohy character (played by Sandra Bullock).

WHERE THERE'S SMOKE, THERE'S GOOD DIALOGUE

Like good black beans, the best dialogue is always smoky. Dialogue exists *between* the lines; keep it subtextual and off-the-nose. We should never be able to hear the writer's voice, only the character's voice.

Take the hit men, Vincent and Jules (played by John Travolta and Samuel L. Jackson), in *Pulp Fiction.* On their way to committing their next murder, they aren't talking about the job, guns, or killing techniques; they're talking about McDonald's Quarter Pounders in America versus McDonald's Burger Royales in Paris, France.

"Big Mac's a Big Mac, but they call it *Le Big Mac.*"

—VINCENT IN *PULP FICTION*

This is wonderful because it reveals the true essences of their characters without dipping into the vast quagmire of clichéd lines that we would usually hear in such a situation. The actors are given lines in which they are able to do what they are paid to do: act. Everything happens between the lines, behind the smokescreen. *Pulp Fiction* jumps off the screen because seemingly ordinary lines are uttered by extraordinary people in extraordinary situations and we never know what's going to be said or what will happen next.

BE ORIGINAL!

Audiences love this originality. And to capture it in your dialogue, don't forget that people don't necessarily answer the questions posed to them. In your next screenplay, try to write a dialogue between your two main characters as two separate monologues woven together; if done properly, the exchange should spring off the page as fresh, original dialogue that seamlessly flows together. Or maybe you want to maintain a sense of discontinuity to demonstrate that, at a certain level, neither of the characters is really listening to the other. As with a good peanut butter and jelly sandwich, you can savor two distinct tastes, but the combination of the two is even better.

The cardinal rule, then, to follow in order to avoid the pitfall of clichéd lines is: be fearless. Take chances with your dialogue. Audiences have been exposed to thousands of hours of television. They want to hear something new. Every time you start writing dialogue and you fall into the trap of writing the first thing that comes to mind—which is usually a boring and/or predictable line of dialogue—instead, try something new and fresh. Try flipping the world around and see what happens. Try having the character say something unexpected or original. For example, just last week, I happened to be sitting next to a nun. Now, what was so wonderful about my interaction with her was that we never once spoke about religion. Instead, our whole conversation was about baseball. It turns out she is a huge Cleveland Indians fan, and it was so fresh and fantastic to hear her talking baseball, especially since she knew a lot more about the game than me. Yes, people are complex. Let their dialogue reflect this complexity.

Give Your Hero a Revelatory Monologue

The second or third act is where the main characters and even some of the leading supporting characters usually have what I call a revelatory monologue (a dramatic speech that reveals their innermost feelings). This monologue makes them three-dimensional. For example, think of the classic speech by Fredo (played by John Cazale) in *Godfather II*, "'You're my younger brother, Mikey, and I was passed over.'" Or Brando's in *On the Waterfront*: "I could have been a contender. I could have been somebody, instead of a bum which is what I am."

Or maybe my all-time favorite revelatory monologue is delivered by Colonel Jessup (played by Jack Nicholson) in Aaron Sorkin's script for *A Few Good Men*. When asked to state the truth by Tom Cruise's character, Jessup replies:

You can't handle the truth! Son, we live in a world that has walls. And those walls have to be guarded by men with guns. Who's gonna do it? You? You, Lieutenant Weinberg? I have a greater responsibility than you can possibly fathom. You weep for Santiago and you curse the Marines. You have that luxury. You have the luxury of not knowing what I know: that Santiago's death, while tragic, probably saved lives. And my existence, while grotesque and incomprehensible to you, saves lives. . . . You don't want the truth. Because deep down, in places you don't talk about at parties, you want me on that wall. You need me on that wall.

And on Jessup goes in an astounding performance of an equally astounding piece of writing. Sure, Jessup might be a bit nuts, but he also makes a hell of a good point. What a wonderful example of exposing the soul of your antagonist in a poetic and moving way.

Or, take Jules's (played by Julianne Moore) revelatory monologue about marriage—given to her wife and two children—in *The Kids Are All Right* (written by Lisa Cholodenko and Stuart Blumberg):

Your mom and I are in hell right now and the bottom line is, marriage is hard. It's really fuckin' hard. It's just two people slogging through the shit, year after year, getting older, changing—fucking marathon, okay? So sometimes, you know, you're together so long you stop seeing the other person, you just see weird projections of your own junk. Instead of talking to each other, you go off the rails, and act grubby, and make stupid choices, which is what I did. And I feel sick about it because I love you guys, and your mom, and that's the truth. And sometimes you hurt the ones you love the most, and I don't know why. You know, if I read more Russian novels ... Anyway ... I just wanted to say how sorry I am for what I did. I hope you'll forgive me eventually. Thank you.

Wow! A hell of a piece of writing, huh? This monologue really takes Jules's character to a new place emotionally. It is moving and powerful to watch and hear, deepens the relationship of all the characters in the story, and forces us all to really think about the nature of marriage—not just gay marriage, but the institution of marriage.

Before we leave this section, I have to add one more monologue, which is actually only a sentence long. Okay, so it's maybe the shortest monologue in history, but it's a damn powerful moment. It's from the film *The Blind Side* and it occurs when Sandra Bullock's character, Leigh Anne Touhy, is sitting with her friends at an upscale restaurant. Her friend Beth says, "You're changing that boy's life." Leigh Anne responds, "No. He's changing mine."

That's it. Four words, but we get in those four words how this young man's presence has completely altered her existence.

In the end, whether your monologues are long or short, they should all be powerful, poignant moments that actors covet, audiences never forget, and the Academy Awards people love to use as clips during their big black-tie self-celebratory hoo-ha.

Where's Judy Garland When You Need Her?

Lastly, the more you hear your dialogue read aloud by actors, the more you will develop an ear for fresh and realistic-sounding language. In most cases, first drafts contain stilted dialogue that is there only for plot reasons. It's your job during the revision process to make your stilted dialogue sing. Having it read aloud can help.

Try visiting your local community theater or university drama classes and asking them to host a reading of your work. If you can't find any actors, have it read aloud by your friends. If you have no friends, read it out loud to yourself.

But, above all, listen to it and you will hear what works. And when you listen, also tune in to what the character does *not* say. This, too, is significant. It reflects an important choice made by the screenwriter. As cerebral thinkers, writers tend to not trust audiences, and think that they have to spoonfeed audiences lots of information. As a result, they tend to overwrite lines of dialogue. Don't fall into this trap. As is true with most things, in the case of dialogue, less is more. Cut, cut, cut. And if you ever are getting nervous about including too few lines of dialogue, always remember, not saying everything allows the audience to inject themselves into the story and fill in the gaps in the dialogue.

Where the Smoke Comes In

The smoke is the silvery screen behind which the characters' true feelings can be masked. In a powerful scene in Robert Redford's excellent film *Quiz Show*, the antagonist and the main character (Rob Morrow and Ralph Fiennes—pronounced, by the way, as "Rafe Fines") play poker. Throughout the scene, they speak only of the game at hand, but it soon becomes clear that when they talk about bluffing and calling, they are really speaking about the quiz show scandal in which they are both deeply and inextricably embroiled.

"Bluffing. The word is bluffing."

—CHARLES VAN DOREN WHEN ACCUSED OF LYING BY DICK GOODWIN IN *QUIZ SHOW*

EXPLOSIONS SPEAK LOUDER THAN WORDS

As we already know, actions can speak louder than words—especially if they are explosions (and we all know how much audiences like things that explode and make lots of noise). Have fun writing your dialogue. Don't become too talky and never forget that the best dialogue is both motivated and restricted by the action of the story.

In real life, few people ever express what they really mean. There are a million ways to say I love you without saying the words "I love you"! And in many cases, the other ways are more effective than the direct one. In fact, sometimes the most powerful way to express information is not through dialogue at all, but through action.

Using Mirrors

Now that you've passed through the smoky part of the screen, it's on to the mirrors section. I use the term "mirrors" because a good revelatory monologue should mirror the inner state of the character. It needn't completely reveal it, for that would contradict our smoke rule, but it should offer a clear reflection. In addition, many times in scripts, especially at the ends of the second and third acts, there are mirror moments—scenes in which the main character hears or sees another character tell about or go through an experience similar to the one the main character is encountering.

"She was the girl, I know that now.
But I pushed her away. So, I've spent every day
since then chasing Amy . . . so to speak."

—SILENT BOB IN *CHASING AMY*

WHEN SILENT BOB SPEAKS

For example, toward the end of *Chasing Amy*, the main character is having girl problems; it is only after Silent Bob (played by the writer, Kevin Smith) finally speaks and tells the protagonist a thematically meaningful story about a time in his life when he chased a girl named Amy. In this story, the main character can see himself clearly reflected and figure out what he needs to do. This mirror moment provides a reflection that allows the main character to see his true state of being more clearly, experience an epiphany of sorts, and move forward to do what needs to be done.

The Wizard's Dialogue Checklist

Here's a checklist of aforementioned items that are components of good dialogue:

1. Be concise (D – ⅓ = 3D).
2. Use artifice, but don't be artificial.
3. Expository dialogue should be buried within scenes rife with conflict and extraneous action.
4. A character must have his or her own distinct voice.
5. Avoid clichéd speech; keep it fresh.
6. Stay smoky, subtle, and subtextual.

7. Remember to give at least one of your characters a good revelatory monologue.

8. Use dialogue to mirror your main character's soul.

From: "Oz" <OzProf@earthmail.com>
To: "Dorothy" <WannaBeScribe@netmail.net>
Subject: Your next exercise

Dear Dot:
As promised, here is your next assignment. Take your time on it.
Wizardly yours,
Oz

Writing Exercise #5

Your assignment is to write a scene in which one character tries to tell another that he or she loves that person without ever using the "L" word. The scene ends with the object of affection demonstrating through action (and maybe subtle dialogue) that he or she either accepts or rejects this love.

Once you have completed this assignment (or if you'd like to try a variation), instead of dealing with love, try writing a scene in which one person tries to reveal to another that a third party has died. Again, the scene ends with the person to whom the revelation is made responding by either accepting or rejecting the knowledge of the death. Go for it. Make artistic choices that are subtle, ambiguous, and interesting without being vague and incomprehensible.

From: "Dorothy" <WannaBeScribe@netmail.net>
To: "Oz" <OzProf@earthmail.com>
Subject: Love, baby . . .

Dear Dr. Wiz.:
Please find that I have chosen to write only the love scene, but rest assured, in it are elements of death, as well.
Hope it exceeds your great expectations,
Pip

Writing Exercise #5 Response

```
INT. JANE'S SUBURBAN HOUSE—NIGHT

JANE, 21, is pacing back and forth. Her brow is wrinkled;
she pouts. The doorbell rings.

Jane opens the door. ERIC, 22, stands in the doorway. He
holds a weed whacker.

                    ERIC
          I came as soon as I could. Here.

                    JANE
          You're a peach.

She grabs it. Eric enters the foyer and walks straight into
the living room.

                    ERIC
          Whacking your weeds, huh?

                    JANE
          You know how it is. The lawn's out of
          control. Have you seen how bad—

                    ERIC
          Hell-llo? Three months ago, it was my
          hedge trimmer. Seven months ago, my
          garden hose—
```

> JANE
> So sue me if I want to take really good
> care of my lawn.

Eric shakes his head in disgust and looks at his watch.

> ERIC
> And Tony, your gardener, will be here
> tomorrow mor—

> JANE
> Yeah, but, I wanted to get a head
> start, before, you know, he—

> ERIC
> He broke up with you, huh?

> JANE
> Tony? No, he's not my type—

> ERIC
> Not Tony . . . Eddie!

> JANE
> Uh-huh. And get this. He did it in a
> text message. Can you believe that?

> ERIC
> Uhhh! What a cowardly bastard!

She puts the weed whacker down. They both sit.

> JANE
> Thanks so much for coming.

> ERIC
> No problem . . . So what am I supposed
> to say now? Oh yeah . . . Here goes:
> (robotic tone) There are other fish in
> the sea. He doesn't deserve you. I never
> liked him anyway. You can do much better!

(Beat)

> How was that?

Jane shoots him an angry glare.

> JANE
> I thought he was the one. You have no
> idea what I'm going through right now.

Eric turns away from Jane and starts to chuckle. He picks up a magazine off of the coffee table and then throws it down in anger.

> ERIC
>
> Oh, bullshit! I bring over lawn care products every time you call and I hope and pray that maybe, just maybe this time, you'll notice me.

> JANE
>
> Don't say it, Eric. Please—

He takes her by the hand.

> ERIC
>
> I don't want to be the consolation prize any more, the Rice-A-Roni. I want to be the brand new Cadillac Escalade. I want the four days and three luxurious nights at the Four Seasons . . .

She understands, pulls her hand away and stands up.

> JANE
>
> Don't worry. You're a very sweet boy. I'm sure you'll find someone.

> ERIC
>
> Yeah, yeah . . . Swell. Thanks.

> JANE
>
> Sorry, but what do you want me to say?

Eric stands up, but keeps his distance.

> ERIC
>
> Never mind. I shouldn't have even bothered to bring it up.

> JANE
>
> Eric, listen. You'll always be my best friend in the whole world.

A moment of silence.

> ERIC
>
> Whoopee.

> JANE
>
> Don't. That's not fair.

                        ERIC
          I know.

Eric grabs his weed whacker.

                        ERIC (Cont'd.)
          Now, if you don't mind, I think I'll
          tend to my own lawn for a while.

Eric turns and walks out. She watches him in silence. A
tear drips down her cheek.

FADE OUT.

THE END.

CHAPTER 9

Genres, as in Family Musical Fantasy Adventure

But that isn't right. The King of Beasts shouldn't be a coward.

"What makes you a coward?" asked Dorothy, looking at the great beast in wonder, for he was as big as a small horse.

"It's a mystery," replied the Lion. "I suppose I was born that way. All the other animals in the forest naturally expect me to be brave, for the Lion is everywhere thought to be the King of Beasts. I learned that if I roared very loudly every living thing was frightened and got out of my way. Whenever I've met a man I've been awfully scared; but I just roared at him, and he has always run away as fast as he could go. If the elephants and the tigers and the bears had ever tried to fight me, I should have run myself—I'm such a coward; but just as soon as they hear me roar they all try to get away from me, and of course I let them go."

"But that isn't right. The King of Beasts shouldn't be a coward," said the Scarecrow.

"I know it," returned the Lion, wiping a tear from his eye with the tip of his tail.

—L. FRANK BAUM, *THE WONDERFUL WIZARD OF OZ*

From: "Dorothy" <WannaBeScribe@netmail.net>
To: "Oz" <OzProf@earthmail.com>
Subject: Genres

For a while now, I've wanted to send you my first draft of my new script, but I was wondering if you might elaborate a bit about genres beforehand, because, well, I'm not sure if it's a thriller or a horror film or a drama or a black comedy, or for that matter, a family musical fantasy adventure. Help! I have a feeling it needs to fit into one of these categories before I go any further.

From: "Oz" <OzProf@earthmail.com>
To: "Dorothy" <WannaBeScribe@netmail.net>
Subject: Generic genres

Dear Pip,
Before I forget, I enjoyed the weed whacker scene. Nice job.
Now, your question about genres is a good one. Yes, storytelling is genre-driven and each genre has demands that must be understood and met. In other words, slow down.

Your Favorite Genre of Genius,
Oz

Film Genres, Inside and Out

Film genres are somewhat fluid categories because they are heavily influenced by the time period and cultural norms at play at the time of the film's production. Though precise causal relationships between films and the culture from which they arise are tenuous, films do reflect the social, political, and economic atmosphere of the time in which they are produced. Those films that reflect most directly (without blinding us, of course) are the ones that the culture ends up embracing. For example, even though many war films deal with conflicts of long ago, they transcend the costume drama genre and stand as covert and sometimes even overt statements about the present American political situation and mood.

Better yet, let us look at sci-fi films such as *Star Trek* and *Avatar*. The fantastic plots of these films may be occurring during some distant time or in some far-off place, but the impetus of the action conveys pointed comments on the political climate of the present day. As the culture changes, so does the nature of the films made by Hollywood within a genre.

Within any genre, there are many variations; yet there are basic elements that characterize each one. Since there are certain requirements that studio readers and audience members consciously and subconsciously expect to be met, the greater the understanding you have of the genre within which you are working, the greater the chance you have of making a sale. Use the following exploration of each of the major genres as a guide to setting your sights before you take aim at your screenplay.

War Films

War films hold a universal appeal because they depict the most basic of all conflicts—the life-and-death battle of man versus man. Yet the singular importance of war films lies in their visions and revisions of old battles in new light. For example, Stanley Kubrick's riveting masterpiece *Full Metal Jacket* provides a counterbalance to the rash of Vietnam War films (*Apocalypse Now*, *Platoon*, *Rambo*, *Missing in Action*, among others) that preceded and romanticized the horror of it. The first half of Kubrick's film depicts the destruction of the soul of the individual and the dehumanization that war and its machinery breeds. The second half of the film illustrates how the newly bred warriors who are "born to kill" wreak havoc and destruction upon the so-called enemy. Kubrick's film attacks the late '70s/early '80s *Rambo* mentality and demythologizes war without employing *Platoon*'s heavy hand.

Another fine example is Ed Zwick's film *Glory*, which represents the work of a modern-day liberal trying his damnedest to rehabilitate the image of the black man in American history. Zwick and screenwriter Kevin Jarre saw the need for a positive portrayal of black soldiers, who have been so important in U.S. military history. They felt that by employing the genre of the historical war melodrama they could redress some of the injustices and .false notions of the past that still prevail today. *Glory* works as both an entertaining war film and also as a valiant attempt to force us to re-evaluate how we think of U.S. history and race. And a movie such as *The Hurt Locker* forces us to look at the recent wars in the Persian Gulf and Iraq.

COMEDIES

The single most important factor that many aspiring writers tend to overlook is this: comedies must be funny. This statement sounds self-evident, but too many writers think that a few clever lines of dialogue or a quirky character make something a comedy, when the reality is that comedy must be based upon an inherently funny premise brought to life with humorous situations. You should not forget to have wonderfully funny characters and dialogue, of course—but it is the larger picture that must be funny first.

Let us begin with the comedic premise. My all-time favorite comedic premise belongs to the classic Mel Brooks film *The Producers*. The concept is simple but brilliant: A film producer, Max Bialystock (played by Zero Mostel), talks to his CPA, Leo Bloom (played by Gene Wilder), and learns that if his next play flops, he can keep all the extra investors' funds. Max woos Leo into becoming a producer and they go about finding the single worst play in history—one that is guaranteed to flop. They produce it with the worst actors they can find, thereby ensuring that their play will fail and they will be able to pocket all the excess funds. Of course, the brilliance of the premise is that the play is so bad that people think it's good, and instead of being a bomb, it turns into a huge hit. This conceit is inherently funny, and with the added pleasures of wonderful actors and Brooks's zany dialogue, we have a true comic treasure.

Start with the premise when writing a comedy. The story must allow for wonderfully rich situations where you can mine comic gold. Be sure to leave room for witty dialogue. But funny lines won't get the truly big laughs unless those funny lines seem to come directly from your characters' personalities. For example, the biggest laugh in radio history came from a huge pregnant pause, not even a spoken word. Jack Benny, whose comedic persona was notorious for being stingy, was held up by a gunman who demanded, "Your money or your life!" Benny's genius lay in his timing, his courage to insert a huge pause between the question and his response. When the robber failed to receive an answer, he prodded Benny, "Well, what'll it be?"

Finally Benny answered, "I'm thinking. I'm thinking!"

On paper, funny; delivered with perfect timing on radio, it becomes hysterical. Take any popular comedy—*The 40 Year Old Virgin, Superbad, The Hangover*—and think about where the laughs are coming from in these films. In almost every case, it's not funny lines, per se, but a combination of character and situation that causes the laugh.

ROMANTIC COMEDIES

The biggest challenge to writing a romantic comedy is the simple fact that almost every plot scenario has been done before. In recent times, it seems as if the best ones have been adventurous enough to find new variations on the traditional theme—boy meets girl, boy loses girl, boy gets girl. Again, we return to premise. How can you vary the premise while still maintaining tension and a conceit that your audience will go along with? *When Harry Met Sally* dealt with the concept of male-female friendships. *Sleepless in Seattle* broke all the rules by having the lovers kept apart for the entire film, which lead to tension and comedy. *(500) Days of Summer* inverted the chronological structure of classic romcoms and moved back and forth in time.

In *My Best Friend's Wedding*, Julianne Potter (played by Julia Roberts) has seventy-two hours to prevent the wedding of her best friend, Michael O'Neal (played by Dermot Mulroney). This is a great premise with a built-in ticking clock. Unfortunately, no matter how likable Julia Roberts tends to be on film, we soon begin to dislike her character since she is acting selfishly and maliciously. However, to the credit of the screenwriter, Ron Bass, she acts unselfishly in the third act. Though this leads to her redemption, it causes a problem for those audience members who don't know what to make of a romantic comedy where the leads are not brought together. As in *Pretty Woman*, where audiences demanded a fairy-tale ending (which was added after test screenings), most audiences have been inculcated to want Richard Gere or whoever the romantic lead is to sweep the heroine off her feet by the final scene of the film.

Your mandate is to find new combinations, twists, and takes, but never to lose sight of the *raison d'être* of romantic comedies— love can conquer all. Yes, love is hard. In many cases, it doesn't work out. If we pay good money to see a romcom, we want the lovers to struggle. We want to think there is no way that they could ever end up together, but in the end, we want them to *be together*. We want to affirm the fact that sometimes true love *can* conquer all. We need to see Julia get her man (*Pretty Woman*), not give him away (*My Best Friend's Wedding*). We want and need our faith in love to be reaffirmed, over and over again.

SCIENCE FICTION/FANTASY

The keys to sci-fi and fantasy films are concept, theme, and special effects (f/x). No one would say that the *Jurassic Park* series is one of the greatest film series ever written. But you can't ignore the fact that it is based upon a successful book, which had a wonderful conceit (what if dinosaur DNA could be genetically engineered to create living, breathing creatures today?), or that it is very well executed both by the writers and the director, or that it dealt with the interesting theme of science versus God, and offered incredibly cool-looking computer-generated images.

We live in an age of technology. Hi-tech films are eye candy that thrills and titillates. Yes, my ticket is expensive, at a cost of $10 or more, but I'm getting to participate in a $120 million Dolby, digital, THX, IMAX, 3-D experience that I would never be able to afford otherwise. If you are James Cameron, you understand this and keep raising the bar with one extravaganza after another. (To his credit, Cameron always seems to care as much about story as f/x, which is, in my mind, the real secret to his great success.)

Now, if you are a writer who cares about story, the rise and pre-eminence of these blockbuster f/x films should trouble you. Yet, as with all titillation, the thrill of eye candy tends to be short-lived, while the need for great stories remains. In other words, once we've seen a specific type of effect, the charm wears off, and the filmmaker must revert to the old mainstays—story and character. No matter how sophisticated the special f/x become, you, the storyteller, will always be needed (at least, for a little while, until the studio owns the script, fires you, and hires a computer graphics team).

In addition to special effects and concept, theme is very important in sci-fi/fantasy films. No matter how far in the past or future the action of your film takes place, or how seemingly fantastic the premise, the theme must be grounded in specific cultural problems of the present day. I would argue that *Independence Day* was so successful because in a world where we often find it exceedingly difficult to get along with other nations, the sight of an alien super-power overrunning our world unites us in a common fight and shows us that, yes, despite what the newspaper might indicate, we can all get along. Or take the *Star Wars* films. *Star Wars* presents a straightforward struggle where good and evil are clearly defined and readily discernible (Luke Skywalker wears white, Darth Vader wears black). We see that sci-fi movies are not just about aliens shooting lasers at each other; they must be well-thought-out stories that are considered on all levels—visual effects, story, and theme. The same, of course, holds true for *Avatar*, which has amazing special effects but would not have made more than $2 billion in box office receipts if the story was not also very powerful and meaningful.

CRIME/GANGSTER PICTURES

This genre will always be present, but it has essentially been played out, at least for now, especially with the rise of the brilliant TV series, *The Sopranos*. And think of this: whatever you write will be compared to the epic *Godfather* trilogy and Martin Scorsese's films. Thus, if you work in this genre, you need to find new variations on the theme. In the '30s and '40s, the antiheroes—Jimmy Cagney, Humphrey Bogart, Robert Mitchum—always received their due and were killed at the end of the picture, proving the theme that crime does not pay. However, as filmmakers desired to convey more complex and ambiguous messages in the '60s through the '80s, they began to complicate their films and the antiheroes did not always end up six feet under.

Take *Goodfellas*. The main character, Henry Hill (portrayed by Ray Liotta), does not face death at the end of the film; instead, he

FOR MORE ON ANTIHEROES

For a wonderful study of the Hollywood antihero or what he calls the outlaw-hero, read Robert B. Ray's *A Certain Tendency of the Hollywood Cinema, 1930–1980*.

must face the prospect of living life as an ordinary schlub like the rest of us. In a way, this is also epitomized in the classic female crime spree film, *Thelma & Louise*. The two antiheroines surely will be killed, but the film fades to white before we see them die.

WESTERNS

Some people say that there are only three truly American art forms—Westerns, the blues, and rock 'n' roll. Even though Westerns are grounded in a specific era in our past (the "manifest destiny" Western expansion era, 1865–1910), new Westerns are constantly being made to speak to our societal problems today.

As our customs and habits change, so does the nature of Westerns. As in gangster pictures, the so-called bad guys in Westerns became complex antiheroes, professionals with whom we empathized and even cheered for when they killed the good guys and survived. For example, think of Billy the Kid in *Young Guns* or the lead characters in *Butch Cassidy and the Sundance Kid*. In the post-Vietnam 1970s, Butch and Sundance don't live, yet in the post-Reagan '90s, Billy the Kid somehow survives. And with Ang Lee's *Brokeback Mountain* and the Coen brothers' Academy Award–winning *No Country for Old Men*, we see further examples of Westerns taking on modern social issues. It is up to you now to figure out how to recast the Western as the world continues to change in the twenty-first century.

FOR MORE ON WESTERNS

For a great study of the structure of Westerns, read a book by Will Wright called *Sixguns and Society*, which gives a detailed analysis of the Western as a reflection of the changes in American culture.

HORROR

To write a horror script, you have to be able to write scenes that scare me so much that I literally have to put the script down to go check and see if the door is locked. You can study the updated rules of the genre by watching the movie *Scream*. One of the most successful of all recent horror films, *Scream* was essentially a take-off on this genre in which Wes Craven, the writer/director, played upon the established conventions of the genre (don't answer the phone, don't walk down a dark hall alone, don't have premarital sex, etc.) and had his characters articulate these rules as they killed each other. Thankfully, it appears as if the rise of the grotesque, gore-filled horror flick as epitomized by the *Saw* series is finally over, praise the Lord.

The other key to horror films is the villain. Freddy, Chucky, and Jason are all whacked-out psychos who have drawn upon fears buried in our psyches, and in doing so have captured our attention and imaginations. Having a compelling villain will, of course, help drive your story, but a film like *Zombieland* demonstrated that having a world of zombies as your villain can also work. This film displayed a unique intelligence and humor that was invigorating, especially compared to all the blood and gore that is predominant in these kinds of films today.

MUSICALS

This form is tricky. The incredible success of the *High School Musical* series and the *Glee* TV series has revitalized a genre once thought deceased, but it still seems like the successes in this genre are more the exception than the rule. Be careful if you tread in this genre, especially if your film is not based upon a successful Broadway property (such as *Chicago*).

True, there are many wonderful old-style musical moments in many recent films. These moments can be used comically, as in the opening song-and-dance sequence from *Austin Powers* or in *The Life of Brian*. No matter what, it is important not to ignore the power of music, whether it is in the form of a song playing in the background (*Pretty Woman*), played on the radio by one of your characters (John Cusack in *Say Anything*), sung by one of your characters (Tom Cruise to Kelly McGillis in *Top Gun*), or sung in unison by a cast of your characters (*Beetlejuice* or *My Best Friend's Wedding*), or a series of songs used to help define character (ABBA in *Muriel's Wedding* or *Mamma Mia*).

Music has become a tremendously significant factor in ticket sales. Soundtracks may get as much recognition as the films they accompany. In fact, in promotional material I saw for the DVD release of *Dead Presidents*, the critic's quote used to advertise the film was not even about the film but about the soundtrack. So don't hesitate to dictate what type of music or even what specific song should play in your scenes.

DOMESTIC MELODRAMAS

This is a genre that many in Hollywood would call "soft" films or character-driven star vehicles. Think *Eat, Pray, Love* and *Julie & Julia* (both of which are based on bestselling books). Formerly called "women's movies," many of these projects are now being quarantined into the world of cable (Lifetime, Oxygen, etc.) and made-for-television movies. What makes these films rise above the movie-of-the-week realm is casting. Get Julia Roberts as your lead and all of a sudden your sensitive tale of a boy who gets cancer and dies young is a big-budget feature (especially since her salary is a good $20 million). All the studios say they are looking for strong character-driven pieces, but be advised: there is a bias against this type of picture as opposed to the so-called event picture (such as *Avatar*). This bias is based on the blockbuster mentality that has taken Hollywood by storm, wherein executives would rather spend $100 or $200 million and pray for a billion-dollar return than spend $15 million for a smaller feature that gives only a $30 million return. (For more information, see Art House/Independent Films.)

ACTION/ADVENTURE

A good spec script in this genre can make agents see dollar signs and repeat the phrase, "ker-ching, ker-ching!" Think *Die Hard*, *Die Hard* on a plane (*Air Force One*), *Die Hard* on a bus (*Speed*), *Die Hard* on a battleship (*Under Siege*), basically *Die Hard* anywhere it hasn't been done so far. Now then, the question arises: This type of script can sell for a lot of money, but only some of these movies make a lot of money—why is that?

The answer is twofold:

1. Film fans like to see movies they like over and over again. Blockbuster films (those that make over $100 million domestic gross) tend to make this type of money from repeat viewers. People go, they like the movie so much they tell their friends, and they go to see the film again *with* their friends.
2. The market for movies these days is international. Much of the total gross for a movie is made overseas, where what counts most is star power and ease of translation.

In essence, this genre, more than all the rest, is based almost completely on visuals. Explosions and car chases play well in any language. In fact, in an interview after the release of one of the *Rambo* films, Stallone stated that he thought a perfect action film would be one that is purely visual and without dialogue. It is your job to feature chases that have never been seen before and new types of explosions that have never been done before. Today, every film seems to be a feeble attempt to outdo that which has come before it and thus we see even bigger explosions and even more ridiculous chase scenes than ever, a la such classics as *The Expendables, Ninja Assassins, The Art of War*, etc.

ART HOUSE/INDEPENDENT FILMS

Essentially, this category captures lower-budget character-driven pieces that do not fit into the high-concept Hollywood mold. However, these are also called Academy Award–winning films, too. For example, the nominees for Best Picture at the Academy Awards in 2010 featured a preponderance of this type of films—*District 9, An Education, The Hurt Locker, Precious, A Serious Man*. Films in this genre are always difficult to get made, especially if they aren't based upon a bestselling book. Write them with a budget in mind. The less costly they are to shoot, the better odds you have of convincing someone to get involved with your project. And with the rise of more affordable technology, it's no longer necessary to spend a fortune to make a film.

Most significantly, this is the genre in which you have the most leeway to say something important about the human condition. One of my favorite examples is Ingmar Bergman's *The Seventh Seal*. In this film, Bergman confronts the central existential issue of finding meaning in life in the face of certain death. As with Job in the Bible, the task of the hero, Antonius Block (Max Von Sydow), is to discover the answer to this eternal question. In 1957, Ingmar

Bergman wrote about what he was trying to do in the program that accompanied the film's release:

> In my film, the Crusader returns from the Crusades as the soldier returns from war today. In the Middle Ages, men lived in terror of the plague. Today, they live in fear of the atomic bomb. The Seventh Seal is an allegory with a theme that is quite simple: man, his eternal search for God, with death as his only certainty.

Antonius Block is fully aware of his own mortality, especially with the omnipresence of the virulent bubonic plague; yet as the film progresses, Block struggles against death and performs at least one meaningful deed before his demise. In so doing, he endows his otherwise meaningless existence with value. *The Seventh Seal* grapples with this complex problem, and Bergman attempts to rectify or at least assuage this existential dilemma.

Whether or not you agree with Bergman's philosophical take on life, you gotta give the guy credit for thinking deeply about existence and trying to speak of our struggles. The key, though, is not to get *too* caught up in cerebral concepts. Even Bergman embodied death (concretized the abstract) as the Grim Reaper and, in doing so, avoided the pitfall of making an overly intellectual and boring film. The film is philosophically significant, and just as important, I feel for Antonius and care about his struggle.

Family Pictures

These used to be called "children's movies," but those marketing geniuses at Disney changed the name to ensure a wider audience than just those under the age of thirteen. Not to be confused with domestic melodramas, family pictures are G-rated comedies or dramas: the sort of picture that Disney was known for and that has reached its apogee with the Pixar masterpieces such as *Wall-E*,

RULES TO WRITE FAMILY PICTURES BY

There are certain components you must include when writing within this genre:

1. The subject can be just about anything as long as it doesn't involve very much vulgar language, realistic violence, or sexual innuendo.
2. There should be a lesson or moral that is conveyed over the course of the action.
3. Don't forget the cute kids and animals, coupled with playfulness and humor. (And ideally, since parents are going to be bringing their children to these films, making clean comedic references to things that go over the kiddies' heads might also be a plus once in a while.)

Even with the downswing in the market for family pictures, with the rise of DVD sales and rentals, there will always be a need for this type of picture, whether it is live action or animated.

The Incredibles, and *Up*. And of course, this genre has produced some timeless classics that seem to constantly spawn sequels that are equally wonderful and successful such as *Toy Story* and *Shrek*.

Some Final Thoughts on Genre

I bumped into a development executive a few years ago, and when we started talking about screenplays, she urged me to consider mixing and matching genres to find new combinations that we have yet to see. Think of how George Lucas conceived of *Star Wars* as a fusion of futuristic sci-fi and old-fashioned Westerns. Just morph Darth Vader's black Stetson into a cool, space-age, black plastic hood and *voilà*, you've got a huge hit!

There is some value to the idea of pushing the boundaries of genres, of trying to reinvent certain genres while still obeying the conventions of that genre. However, always, please be careful—too much blending without regard for the inherent requirements of the genres can lead to an unsatisfying mix of something that I like to call a flying fish. A flying fish is neither as satisfying as a bird of the air or a fish of the sea but a strange hybrid that doesn't seem to really fit in either the air or the sea. Audiences want peanut butter and jelly or peanut butter and marshmallow fluff, but nobody likes jelly and fluff.

From: "Oz" <OzProf@earthmail.com>
To: "Dorothy" <WannaBeScribe@netmail.net>
Subject: Generic

Okay then, I hope all your generic questions have been answered and your generic angst has been quelled.

Generically your,

Ozzie

CHAPTER 10

Writing Is Rewriting

The Tin Woodman took great care never
to be cruel or unkind to anything.

But the Scarecrow seized the oil-can from Dorothy's
basket and oiled the Woodman's jaws, so that after a few
moments he could talk as well as before.

"This will serve me a lesson," said he, "to look where
I step. For if I should kill another bug or beetle I should
surely cry again, and crying rusts my jaws so that I cannot speak."

Thereafter he walked very carefully, with his eyes on
the road, and when he saw a tiny ant toiling by he would
step over it, so as not to harm it. The Tin Woodman knew
very well he had no heart, and therefore he took great
care never to be cruel or unkind to anything.

"You people with hearts," he said, "have something to
guide you, and need never do wrong; but I have no heart,
and so I must be very careful. When Oz gives me a heart
of course I needn't mind so much."

From: "Dorothy" <WannaBeScribe@netmail.net>
To: "Oz" <OzProf@earthmail.com>
Subject: And away we go . . .

Dear Harsh Slave-Driver Whom I Worship and Adore:
I think you just saved me twelve drafts. My new script is definitely a romantic comedy and I have now altered it accordingly to ensure that it fits within the confines of your clearly defined generic parameters. THANKS!

Your loving disciple,
The Great Conformist

P.S. As you may have guessed, the first draft of my script is done and is attached. Hope it strikes your fancy and doesn't need numerous rewrites. And if you don't want to read it, feel free to delete or once again toss it into your laptop's recycle bin.

From: "Oz" <OzProf@earthmail.com>
To: "Dorothy" <WannaBeScribe@netmail.net>
Subject: The fine art of revision

My Little Conformist:
Your new script is a wonderful read—especially for a first draft.
I would never tell you how many drafts to write, but I would recommend a series of rewrites. You must start to develop the maturity to realize that, yes, there is value to artistic freedom, but film is a collaborative medium and we must engage in the process.
And the key to the process is rewriting.

Yours, over and over again,
The King of the Rewrite

Learn to Love the Rewrite

The main thing that separates award-winning writers from everyone else is their ability to rewrite. Everyone's first drafts need work. Great writers know what work needs to be done and spend the hours and days and months (or even years) necessary to revise their work so that all its many facets shine. They etch and carve and polish it until their work gleams. And they know what to eliminate and what to keep.

That's the key: Changing the *right* stuff . . . .

So how do you develop the expert vision to see what should be kept in and what should be cut? The answers lie in an understanding and exploration of the process of revision.

Pay No Attention to the Writer Behind the Curtain . . . or Screen

The first thing to remember about rewriting is that *it ain't about you*. It's about the story! It is your job to get out of the way of the story and do whatever it takes to let the story shine through with truth and beauty. And since screenwriting is a transitional medium while other forms of writing like poetry and fiction are terminal art forms, it's especially important that your story speaks its messages clearly.

Let me explain. When a poet or novelist finishes her work of art, it is served whole, exactly as she composed it, to her audience. We read her poem or novel and, hopefully, we get exactly what she wanted to convey to us. Thus, I call it a terminal art form, since when it is done, it is done. But screenwriting is a transitional art form, since the script is merely a blueprint for a greater work of art that includes the collaboration of many others. So, the script, when done, is not really finished, but merely a starting point. It is a transitional work designed to inspire further art.

That's one reason why writing, and especially screenwriting, is not a medium designed for showoffs. The audience never cares how smart you are or how clever or how good your vocabulary or sentence structure is. Sure, the story starts with you, but it ends with a lot of other people contributing, so get over yourself. It's not about you. Hence, as the Wizard does in Baum's masterpiece, you need to stay happily hidden behind a screen or curtain. Yes, of course, you are pulling the strings to get the story going, but you must remain hidden.

If this is a problem for you, give up screenwriting and become an actor.

If this isn't a problem, and you are fine with putting the story first and putting your ego second, this whole rewrite process will become much easier.

No One Is Exempt—and That Means You!

And so we consider the nature of rewrites. Everyone needs to do them, no matter how experienced or infamous you are. I won't venture to say exactly how many drafts you should write before you show a screenplay to Hollywood professionals, but I would recommend conducting a long series of revisions. For some, this might mean three drafts, for others thirteen, and for others, thirty-three. Remember, the first draft is merely a start; the characters, themes, and plot are not fully fleshed out until you do a series of other drafts.

WHEN IS *THE END* THE END?

Engaging in a series of drafts is not something to be ashamed of, but a natural discipline that you must endure. The real question that inevitably arises is not How much longer must I keep going, but When should I stop?

Oscar Wilde was right. I don't want to see you turn into Frederick Jackson Turner, who, after having sold a painting he wasn't completely satisfied with to the Royal Gallery in England's Palace

"Art is never finished, it is merely abandoned."

—OSCAR WILDE

of Westminster twelve years earlier, couldn't take it any more. He snuck into the room one day, paint and brush hidden in his coat, in order to make the painting right. Turner needed to let go, but you, my dear, are far from that place. I believe you are still a series of drafts away from abandonment or immortalization in a museum.

Write a Feverish First Draft

In her wonderful book *Bird by Bird*, Anne Lamott talks about the need for writers to not be afraid of "shitty first drafts." I agree with her. First drafts are about getting the work out of your head, and nothing else. If you are too focused on a perfect first draft, the odds are you will never even finish it. However, instead of thinking of shitty first drafts, I like to encourage my students to write feverish first drafts. Feverish because, like a virus that infects the system, the initial spurt of inspiration causes the body's temperature to rise and then must run its course if it is to be flushed out of the system. Likewise, a first draft must be produced in a feverish delirium or it might never appear.

First You Go Wild

There are two aspects to writing: call it right-brain/left-brain, call it creating/revising, visceral/cerebral, or heart/mind. Call it any duality that you want, but know that the first draft involves the act of creation. It should be freeform; let your mind go wild. Do not judge yourself, and avoid that internal self-censor who paralyzes you. Find your story and get it out of your head. Stop worrying about quality: It's just your rough draft. It doesn't count. It's just brainstorming on paper. It's the beginning, not the end.

THEN, YOU FIX IT

Then, after that no-holds-barred rushing forward, creative, right-brain, feverish first draft has poured out of you, lean in the opposite direction and allow that anal-retentive, left-brain, OCD editor to take over and do its job. Let order become the rule of the day. Develop your rough draft into a highly polished gem of a script. Work it, work it, *work* it, until it is a thing of beauty.

Find a Constructive Critic

To develop your stories and scripts, at some point you are going to need help from others. These others may be teachers, other writers, or even paid script consultants. They should be offering *constructive,* not destructive, criticism of your work. That means that they are contributing ideas on how to improve scenes and revealing problems in your script to which you were previously blind, and not just telling you, "This doesn't work for me . . . Not sure why, but something's not right."

CRITIQUE YOUR CRITICS

If you are getting help from others, learn to critique your critics. Be especially careful of letting loved ones read your work. Remember to ask yourself, Who exactly is giving me this feedback? What is his or her agenda? What is yours? Who is the audience for your work? Is your critic part of your audience? Is he or she offering thorns or roses? Tainted, wilted lettuce or vitamin-filled spinach that will enrich your story the same way it fills Popeye with strength?

Unfortunately, many so-called writing teachers are frustrated never-has-beens who maintain their tenuous authority by knocking aspiring writers down, thereby building themselves up. Or even worse, they are petty, competitive writer wannabes who are jealous of your tenacity and offer mean-spirited criticism in a covert effort to break you down and crucify you. Ask yourself the questions in the previous paragraph to see if your teacher is a helpful, encouraging one—or not.

With practice and experience, you will be able to sort through all the comments and know which ones are helpful and which are not. Once you do, pay heed to the criticism that is on the mark. Yes, your skin will have had to congealed and thickened to a crusty hardness—again, it's all part of the process. Even if at first you thought some of the feedback was self-serving and wrong-headed, do not misdirect your personal frustrations toward your critic; this is wrong and unfair. If they have taken the time to offer you constructive feedback and it corresponds to other feedback you have received, it is time to stop being defensive and to start the painstakingly hard work of revision.

WRITE IT OUT

True, this process is incredibly painful. The only way to numb the hurt is to turn your laptop back on and start in on your rewrites. The very act of writing should make you feel a whole lot better.

You should prioritize rewrites just as you did your original writing. Some writers get off track here and spend too much time networking to sell their script at this point. Even though attempts at networking are a significant part of the business, they are not the most important part. Too much time spent away from your writing becomes an act of avoidance. Writing is what you need to do and, in the end, it seems to be the only thing that truly heals the wounds that criticism can bring. So, dig your heels in and revise!

To Your Second Draft—and Beyond!

With the second draft and beyond, the real work begins. In art, as in life, you are judged by the choices you make. You must reach a level of self-awareness whereby you intuitively know what to add and what to take out. Be honest enough with yourself to accept that there are elements of your work that are weak. Then, consciously eliminate these elements until you have a series of scenes that work (they should be a series of fresh and original moments that organically flow together and advance the story, as well as communicate the theme).

As in any ballgame, when we start, the score is zero–zero. The best writers have the ability to transcend the field; they know what

 # FINGERPAINTING FOR GROWNUP SCREENWRITERS

Consider the kindergarten art teacher who consistently has wonderful fingerpainters in her class. She achieves this year after year, not because she is a better teacher or has better students, but because she encourages them to paint whatever they want and she knows exactly when to pull the painting away from them before they make a muddy brown mess. Like this teacher, you must learn to recognize when your colors are most vivid, and when too much color will serve only to obscure your art.

it takes to win. But they are not really any different than you and me. They are not superhuman; they are merely people who have trained themselves over the years to make the right choices. They know when to keep writing and when to stop.

Apply the Final Polish

The remaining drafts and the final polish require the skills of revising, editing, and re-creating—that is, imposing order upon the disorderly chaos of art. And if the story is dragging, ask yourself, what is at stake? And then raise the stakes!

The Final Polish Checklist

Here are some questions to ask yourself as you wind down your series of revisions:

1. Does your antagonist (or antagonists) appear to be stronger than the good guy?
2. Does your main character have a strong arc? Is he or she the type of role an actor is going to want to play?
3. Do any lines of your dialogue or any of your scenes feel like a cliché? If so, fix them! What can you do to make each line of dialogue and every scene feel original or quirky?
4. Do you have a strong climax?
5. Does every scene push the story forward? And does each scene start at the last possible second and end as soon as possible? (In other words, did you get into the scene as late as possible and get out as soon as possible?)

The final draft must embody the union of your creative impulses and the rational structures you have imposed upon them. Think of it as a merger of form and function. Body and soul. Yin and yang. Abbott and Costello.

Imbed a Microstory

One way to deepen your script as you revise is to include a microstory that echoes the film's theme. "Microstory" is a term I coined for any type of tale, parable, allegory, anecdote, myth, or legend told within the context of the larger plot of the film. Not to be confused with a subplot, a microstory usually signifies to the audience what they will be getting from the movie as a whole—i.e., the main theme.

Many times, microstories are told in pre-credit sequences, as in *The Blind Side*, when the story of the great New York Giants linebacker, Lawrence Taylor, is told as a way of developing the theme of the importance of the "blind side" offensive lineman in the modern game of football. In other films, a microstory is told by a character in the story, as illustrated by the legend of the tree in *Avatar*. In *The Wizard of Oz* book, there are many microstories, but one of my favorites is the Tin Woodman's tale of how he came to be of tin and without a heart. In *To Kill a Mockingbird*, of course, it is the tale of the mockingbird told by Atticus.

 TALK UP YOUR MICROSTORY

If you are having trouble finding your story, microstory, or theme, try talking it out. During preproduction, Hitchcock used to tell the story of the movie he was going to make to everyone he met. This act of telling and retelling your story helps you constantly refine it and determine exactly what your story is about and what you are trying to say with your story.

Choose Your UFD

In many scripts, certain key thematic elements or motifs serve as a sort of author's or auteur's signature. I call these signatures unifying filmic devices (UFDs)—never to be confused with UFOs or STDs, please. UFDs are not essential to your storytelling, but when they are present, they add an extra level of meaning that can deepen and unify your film.

For example, in *The Graduate*, water imagery serves as the UFD. Ben (played by Dustin Hoffman) is first seen through a fishtank. His relationship with his parents is symbolized by his efforts to surface out of the pool in his scuba suit and their repeated attempts to push him back in the water, and the climax takes place in a huge glass church that looks like—yep, you guessed it—a large aquarium.

UFDs are everywhere in film and can have great power, even if that power is not something that the audience consciously perceives. For example, consider the 2010 film *The Karate Kid* starring Jaden Smith and Jackie Chan. In this film, one sees the main character, Dre Parker, constantly leaving his jacket on the ground. This then becomes a key element, a UFD, signifying the development of his character. Han, played by Jackie Chan, uses Dre's jacket as a training tool and Dre learns fundamental kung fu moves by picking his jacket up off the ground over and over again. Sure, it's just a jacket, but picking it up over and over again actually becomes a symbolic gesture of his growth as a martial artist and human being.

Probably my favorite example of the use of UFDs is by the great director Alfred Hitchcock in his masterpiece, *Psycho*. In this film, Hitchcock's composer, Bernard Herrmann, chose to use high-pitched, birdlike screeching in his soundtrack to link the bird imagery with Hitchcock's characterizations. Thus, we have two UFDs working together: birdlike sounds and bird imagery.

The opening shot of the film is a bird's-eye view of Phoenix, Arizona, mixed with a romantic musical theme played by stringed instruments. Throughout *Psycho*, Hitchcock mixes bird imagery and harsh birdlike screeching to create fear and confusion in the audience—fear because they anticipate violence when they hear it, and confusion because they associate the bird music with Norman Bates's supposedly homicidal mother, even though they should really associate it with Norman, a collector of stuffed birds.

In the famous shower/murder scene, the audience sees Mrs. Bates (Norman in drag) open the shower curtain and hears a series of sounds mixed together: first, the curtain rips open, a steam whistle screeches, Janet Leigh screams in terror, the knife stabs her body; and then we hear the now-famous high-pitched bird screeching musical motif played by the string section of the orchestra. As a result of the soundtrack, the audience feels much more terror and also associates the music with Norman, his mother, and the stuffed birds.

The shower scene also refers back to the scene of Janet Leigh driving her car through the pouring rain. In this scene, Hitchcock uses the bird music motif to add tension. He also focuses his camera on the windshield wiper blades, which look like shiny talons or knives cutting through the water. These are a direct reference to Norman's knife, which will cut through Janet Leigh's wet body later in the film.

Even the scenery at the Bates Motel is filled with birds—both painted pictures and Norman's stuffed collection. The birds represented in the motel are not joyous birds of flight, but ominous birds of prey. Hitchcock endows these birds with a dark, predatory air, so that upon seeing them, the audience grows tense and scared. Even Norman is shot in dark shadow in such a way that he becomes birdlike in appearance, his nose a beak, his jaws chewing on food like a bird trying to crack open its meal.

Hitchcock and Herrmann skillfully construct a masterpiece of the horror genre by employing a unifying visual motif of birds accompanied by a unifying musical motif of birdlike screeching music. Together, these elements demonstrate Hitchcock's and Herrmann's genius by affecting the audience more profoundly than either one of these UFDs could have alone.

WHERE'S YOUR UFD?

Now, look at your script. If you haven't already put at least one UFD into your screenplay, find one and weave it throughout your script. It should add that extra layer that could make the difference between a good read and a great one.

Ready, Aim, Rewrite!

If you have covered all your bases and abided by the lessons I have mentioned in this and previous chapters, you may be almost ready to send out your script. Take it easy there, and please remember, there is no rush. Take your time and keep plugging away. *Re*write, rewrite, and then rewrite some more.

Never submit too early. You only get one chance. So when you are finally convinced your screenplay is ready to go out, resist the temptation, seal it up in an envelope, and stick it in a safety deposit box for a week. After your mandatory seven days have expired, pick it up, reread it, and if you are still convinced it is perfect, then yes, you can send it out.

From: "Dorothy" <WannaBeScribe@netmail.net>
To: "Oz" <OzProf@earthmail.com>
Subject: The best spec script ever

Dear Ozzie:
Thank you so much. Owing to your tutelage, I have finally revised and finished my script. (Hallelujah!) I am convinced it is the best thing I have ever written. I have sent a copy as a PDF attachment. I am so excited. I know it is the high-concept type of spec script that bidding wars are made of.
Hope you enjoy reading it as much as I enjoyed writing it.

All the best,
Ecstatic Tin Woodman

From: "Oz" <OzProf@earthmail.com>
To: "Dorothy" <WannaBeScribe@netmail.net>
Subject: Whoa, Nellie . . .

Dear Hyper One:
Relax.
I wish I could sing the praises of your little opus and distribute it to all my cronies, but I still don't think it's ready. I hope you have not sent it out anywhere. Go back and read my instructions on revisions and keep working at it.

Write back soon,
Trying to Help

From: "Dorothy" <WannaBeScribe@netmail.net>
To: "Oz" <OzProf@earthmail.com>
Subject: Wicked

Dear Wicked Witch:

I'm sorry, but I have to get this off my chest. Are you really trying to help, or are you trying to maintain your tenuous authority base by pushing me down and building yourself up? I mean, because you're burned out and have unresolved issues, do you think that justifies your efforts to try to stifle me?

If you haven't already figured it out, I've spent over a year on my script and frankly, I'm hurt and saddened that you would feel the need to compete with me instead of helping me.

I thought you were different, but I guess you're no better than the rest of them.

Outraged and Saddened

From: "Oz" <OzProf@earthmail.com>
To: "Dorothy" <WannaBeScribe@netmail.net>
Subject: Sorry, but . . .

Dear Outie:

Until you grow up, I think our correspondence should be discontinued.
The Wicked Witch

CHAPTER 11

The Business of Show

The Emerald City ain't really green.

"I found myself in the midst of a strange people, who, seeing me come from the clouds, thought I was a great Wizard. Of course I let them think so, because they were afraid of me, and promised to do anything I wished them to.

"Just to amuse myself, and keep the good people busy, I ordered them to build this City, and my palace; and they did it all willingly and well. Then I thought, as the country was so green and beautiful, I would call it the Emerald City, and to make the name fit better I put green spectacles on all the people, so that everything they saw was green."

"But isn't everything here green?" asked Dorothy.

"No more than in any other city," replied Oz; "but when you wear green spectacles, why of course everything you see looks green to you."

—L. FRANK BAUM, *THE WONDERFUL WIZARD OF OZ*

From: "Dorothy" <WannaBeScribe@netmail.net>
To: "Oz" <OzProf@earthmail.com>
Subject: My deepest apologies

Dear Prof.:
Sorry . . .
Sorry, sorry, sorry.
I have been quite depressed and misdirected some of my personal frustrations toward you, which is wrong and unfair. So now, I've picked my script back up, re-evaluated it, and I see that, yes, there are still quite a few problems. Okay, fine, yes, you were right.

Again, I'm sorry.
Repentant and Unworthy

P.S. If this script is ever ready, do you have any recommendations as to the whole business of selling scripts, agents, and the like?

From: "Oz" <OzProf@earthmail.com>
To: "Dorothy" <WannaBeScribe@netmail.net>
Subject: This wacky business we call show

Dear Kneeling One:
Apology accepted.
As per your request for info about the business of screenwriting, here goes nothing, and I mean, nothing.

Yours truly,
Show Biz Wiz

A Look Back . . .

To truly understand the film business, you should start by looking at its history. According to the *U.S. Statistical Abstract*, in 1930 weekly cinema attendance was around 80 million people, approximately 65 percent of the resident U.S. population. However, by 2000, it was only 27.3 million people, which was 9.7 percent of the U.S. population at that time.

This, of course, means that the films of the 1930s and 1940s were seen by a huge percentage of the American population. During that time, movies were a vital part of American culture. With the rise of TV in the 1950s and other forms of mass entertainment, those numbers kept dwindling. David Thomson, in an *Esquire* magazine article in August 1977, stated, "[O]ver the past seven decades as America's population has doubled, the number of movie tickets sold yearly has fallen by half."

The movie industry was struggling. It wasn't really until 1975 with the release of *Jaws* that things started to change. Essentially, the triumvirate of Steven Spielberg, George Lucas, and Francis Ford Coppola resuscitated the industry. Blockbusters with megagrosses were the new saviors-on-the-block. Movies, especially summer and Christmas blockbusters, were back with a vengeance. In order to compete with other media and win back their wandering audience, films had to be bigger, faster, and cooler, with more explosions, death, sex, and special effects than ever before.

That is why you need to find indie finance for your sweet, small script, but Twentieth Century Fox was willing to spend $200 million on *Avatar*. With this understanding of the marketplace in mind, let us now look at how to jam your beloved spec script between the frame and door without getting your fingers crushed.

Find Your Own Way in the Enchanted Forest

When mythologist and author Joseph Campbell spoke of medieval mythology, he often mentioned that a young knight could not follow the established path in the woods as he ventured forth on his quest. Instead, each knight had to blaze a new trail, his own path through the dark woods.

This is the key metaphor for each individual's lifelong journey toward a healthy psyche and identity—and for each screenwriter's attempt to make it in Hollywood. We each must make our own way through the treacherous Hollywood jungle. Yes, there are some well-trodden trails, but they quickly get overgrown with dense foliage, and even if they led to large chunks of gold ore for others before you, there is no guarantee that you will have the same luck.

However, the longer you keep searching, blazing new trails, dipping your pan in the river, the better chance you have of coming up with a few nuggets of gold. That is, of course, if you are consistently following your instincts and conscientiously learning from your mistakes, not just methodically and blindly panning the same area over and over again.

Schmoozing 101

While metaphors such as the previously mentioned trailblazing gold-panner can sometimes help clarify the business of screenwriting, the reality of Hollywood is such that sometimes it seems that success is as much about schmoozing as it is about writing. First and foremost, it is always what is on the page that counts. But if a studio executive or an agent has to choose between a shlumpy, antisocial, inarticulate shmuck and a well-groomed, highly articulate type who seems capable and handles himself well in meetings, guess who is going to get the writing assignment? Never forget:

people, when given a choice, would rather work with a friend than an enemy or stranger.

Yep, screenwriting is not just an art and a craft; it is also a business. No matter how well you write, you cannot afford to be a pure *artiste*, sitting in your loft, chain-smoking and looking down upon the rest of us with disdain. You have to be able to sell yourself on the page, on the phone, and in person. Once someone likes your script, she has to like you and want to spend hours and hours huddled in a room with you, revising it. So guess what? All that work you have done developing yourself as a human being as well as a writer may finally pay off.

It's Not Over till the Fat Producer Sings

Let's start at the beginning. A screenplay is truly finished only when it is sold and/or produced, and this will never happen unless you get the work read by industry professionals.

Novice screenwriters are inevitably afraid to share their work because they're afraid someone will steal their story. Yes, I'm talking cold-blooded thievery. The false, illegal, and heartless grabbing of your work by another (usually an oily, sleazy, and conniving type) without credit or remuneration. Does it really happen? Sure. Does it happen a lot? No. Should it stop you from ever submitting your work? No! What can you do to keep it from happening to you?

You can start by registering your script with the Writers Guild of America (7000 W. 3rd St., Los Angeles, CA 90048, 213-782-4500, *www.wga.org*) and/or the Copyright Office (Library of Congress, Washington, D.C., 20059, 202-707-3000, *www.loc.gov*). But alas, you can't register *ideas*. So if you write a great script about a talking zebra, someone could change it to a talking giraffe and there's nothing you can do about it except go to the zoo and curse at all the giraffes you meet.

In the end, you have to believe that it's cheaper for them to hire an unknown like you for Writers Guild minimum than to steal your idea and pay a heavy hitter the big bucks to do what you have already done for them at a fraction of the cost.

If you submit your work to an agent or producer and they ask you to submit a waiver before they read it, you really have no choice but to sign. (The waiver basically says that you are waiving your rights to sue them if they do a project similar to yours.) It's okay; life is full of risks. Your script ain't gonna do anybody any good sitting there on your nightstand collecting cobwebs and coffee stains.

Go ahead. Take a chance. Put it out there and pray.

The Better to Represent You, My Pretty

Now, on to the wacky, wonderful world of agents. It is rumored that, years ago, agents would foster young talent. They would take on an unknown based on the possibility that he might turn into the next Shane Black or William Goldman. These days, the agents I meet just don't seem to have the time or energy to do this. They are under the gun to make as much money as possible and maintain a huge client load. All they want are commercially viable scripts that they can sell immediately. It is a game of instant gratification, not long-term artistic growth. Unless you come highly recommended or already have a track record and representation, they probably won't be interested in you. Thus, the Catch-22 of the Hollywood world: I can't get my script out there if I don't have an agent, yet I can't get an agent unless I have stuff that is already out there! Is Hollywood a great town or what?

IT SIZZLES WHEN IT'S HOT, DOT

Welcome to the nonsensical pleasures of La-La Land. I have come to believe that it is almost impossible to get an agent unless they come after you. So then, you must create your own mystique, aura, heat, and sizzle, so that they come looking for you.

How do I create sizzle, you may ask? Well, there is no one correct answer.

First, if you know anyone—a teacher, friend, family member, cousin, distant relative—who is represented, have that person make a recommendation and then follow up on it. You might also consider a literary manager, who does essentially the same thing as an agent—but they get 15 percent, not 10 percent, and he or she can also be a producer. This might be a good thing, but also could be problematic, depending on whether the literary manager as producer weighs your project down or adds value to it. No matter what, please note that an agent can't ever produce.

If you don't have any recommendations, create your own heat by attaching yourself to something that agents might want. This could be anything, no matter where in the world you may live. Here are some ideas:

- ✧ Make a film and enter it in festivals. There are literally hundreds of film festivals around the world these days. Many cater to specific types of films, so the right one to enter might be a function of what kind of film you've made. A few prestigious festivals include Sundance, Toronto, South by Southwest, Slamdance, and Telluride.
- ✧ Get the rights to a book or a hot topic featured in a magazine article by trying to contact the author of the book or article. Many times, this will not be easy and you might have to deal with agents or lawyers or publishing houses. However, it is easier than ever to reach people today via social media networks and the Internet, so it is worth trying to go directly to the author and see if he is interested. If he is, try to get an option on his material and get a good lawyer to help you negotiate this all.

✧ Comb through agent/manager directories. There are many lists on the Internet of reputable agents and managers who help writers get their work out into the world. But please note, most writers reach out to agents and managers before they and their script are ready. There is no rush. Make sure your script is the very, very best it can be before trying to contact someone to represent you.

THE HOLLYWOOD CREDO

Before we go any further, I'd like to stress the fact that to truly understand agents, you need to understand a basic credo upon which almost everything in Hollywood is hinged: There are only two types of people in this town—those who create something from nothing (writers) and those who build upon that creation (actors, directors, agents, lawyers, producers, development executives). The majority of people, no matter how talented they are at doing their jobs, have to attach themselves to those who can create.

FOR THE PURE OF HEART

If you fancy yourself a pure writer (big mistake)—one who fantasizes about doing nothing else but staying at home and working—having representation is essential.

FOR THE REST OF US

Many times, deals for most writers (even those with representation) happen as a result of their own efforts on behalf of their projects, not from agency connections.

Go out there and keep peddling your stuff. And always remember, the numbers you hear about big-dollar script sales can be deceptive. Think about it. If you were to sell a project, here are a few of the people who would get a cut: manager, 15 percent; agent, 10 percent; lawyer, 5 percent; the good old U.S. Government, 40 percent. What's left for you, the writer? You do the math, Scarecrow.

Still, representation can be a good thing to complement what you are already doing for your own career. Be judicious in who you ally yourself with. If you do get a bite from a potential agent, judge the person by his enthusiasm and excitement for your work, and remember: In the end, you are your own number-one client, and no one cares about you and your work as much as you do. The reality is that *you* will generate most of the work you get, no matter how good your representation may be or how many doors he has opened for you.

Let me give you a more specific example. Let's say you bust your hump on a project for two years, and then sell it for what seems like a lot of money, the whopping sum of $100,000. After all is said and done, what do you have to show for yourself at the end of the day? $30,000 divided by two years' worth of work, which equals $15,000 a year. You could have been making more money flipping burgers at MacWendy's. But that doesn't mean you have to give it all up and say, "Screw it, let the maggots find another host. I don't want the vampires sucking the creative juices out of me." Just be conscious of this reality and don't enter the business with cash registers ringing in your ears.

Swimming with the Hollywood Sharks

Yes, the agent track is a dubious one filled with pitfalls. However, if you are fortunate enough to reach an agent who accepts unsolicited manuscripts, whether you've made contact over the phone or by e-mail, send your script as a PDF via e-mail. Then wait a week or two, and e-mail to see if he has received it. Then wait a few more weeks and if you still haven't heard from him, e-mail once a week and ask politely if he has gotten to it yet.

If you write or call more than once a week, you're getting dangerously close to becoming a nuisance. If you write or call less often than once a week, the agent might forget about you. If he does express interest, and maybe even, God forbid, sign you, remember, agents are not demigods. You still have to keep working on your craft and you are not your agent's only client. Don't stop writing and spend your life sitting around, waiting. Make things happen for yourself, and then bring the agent in to help negotiate your deal.

REPPING YOURSELF

If you are running into a brick wall in the agency world, there are alternatives. You are allowed to climb over the agency stepladder and head directly to production companies. Sure, it's difficult, but it's possible. There are several ways to go about it.

Get a Lawyer

First of all, there are tons of Hollywood lawyers and managers who are always searching for good scripts to get their paws on and push around town. If they do, rest assured, they will take a commission (a percentage of your fees—lawyers usually get 5 percent, managers, 15) or a producer credit; so make sure you are clear as to the arrangement before you allow one of them to go out with your project.

Read the Hollywood Creative Directory

This handbook is fairly expensive (it is available at any Samuel French location or online at *www.samuelfrench.com*), but it lists the contact info for the players at every major studio and many independent production companies. So, if you have written the perfect vehicle for Sandra Bullock, you can look up her production company and e-mail them. Remember, your e-mail query should be concise—just write a few sentences about the story and about you. That's it—don't write more than a computer screen's worth of information. Hook them with a good subject line and let them decide if it's something of interest.

Sure, you might get stonewalled, rejected, and/or ignored. But these companies always need product for their clients, so there is always a chance that when you e-mail them, they will express interest.

Go Online

Here are some legitimate websites that might be helpful as you try to get your work out to the world:

❖ *www.donedealpro.com*
❖ *www.equerydirect.com*
❖ *www.inktip.com*
❖ *www.screenwriting-source.com*

At least this is what my students claim. I am not involved with self-marketing via the Internet and I want to stay that way.

However, if and when you do use web resources, rest assured that everyone and his mother is also constantly e-mailing agents and entertainment lawyers and managers and producers, trying to get them to read their scripts. So, if you do reach out electronically, try to differentiate yourself from the thousands of others who are also out there sending e-mails to each and every Hollywood figure they can contact. If you wrote a script about a fireman and you were a fireman for ten years, make sure to mention that. Make sure your e-mail is well-written and addressed to the right person. Be professional; only offer a complete, revised script; and be patient!

Netflix It

Another potential route is to log on to Netflix.com and take a virtual stroll through films that are similar to your project. Of course, you can do a similar search on IMDB.com for free. Or,

TIME OUT FOR BUSINESS

Whatever happens, always dedicate a portion of your day—whether it is ten minutes or two hours—to the business of being a professional writer (e-mails, phone calls, follow-ups, pursuing leads, and the like).

And please, pace yourself. If your e-mails have gotten ignored day after day, stop and start again a week later. Too much rejection can be bad for the psyche.

for a minimal monthly investment, you might look into joining IMDbPro, which offers even more information, especially about projects in development. Whether you join Netflix or IMBbPro, or just surf the net, look at the credits and note the production companies involved in projects that are similar to what you are working on. Find the names and numbers or e-mail addresses of the people you might want to talk to. Odds are they won't be easy to contact and/or to get to respond to you, but how will you ever know for sure unless you find out?

Dorothy Does the Meet & Greet

If you do get a bite, and an agent or manager calls you in for a little "meet & greet" pitch session, go in upbeat, friendly, cordial. Don't start by immediately talking about your project. Talk about a movie you've seen recently. Talk about the Dodgers. Show them that you can do more than write and you are interested in other things besides writing. Don't be negative.

When you get to your pitch, have tremendous enthusiasm for your project. If you don't, how can you expect them to? Most executives suffer from attention deficit disorder and none seem to have discovered Ritalin, so make it brief and colorful. And if it ain't working, don't push it. Pull in the reins. Throw out a different idea. If they're unreceptive, get out when the getting's good. Don't overstay your welcome and don't fret if you get no response.

In any and all business relations, choose your fights. Yes, there are times to stand up for what you believe, but film is a commercial, collaborative medium. Never forget this.

Over the years I have talked to many successful writers, and when they are not complaining about how directors and producers have bastardized their work, it seems to me that the common bond among them is a tendency to avoid trying to maintain complete control over every single tiny aspect of their work. Will it kill you to lose that character or scene or line? Probably not. Keep things in perspective if someone offers a suggestion like that.

 # THERE'S NO PLACE LIKE HOME

An old friend of mine, the late, great screenwriter Stirling Silliphant, Academy Award winner for *In the Heat of the Night* and the first man to be paid a million dollars for a script, once told me that the biggest mistake he ever made was moving to Beverly Hills. He said that once he committed to the big house and the 90210 lifestyle, it destroyed his writing career by forcing him to take assignments for money instead of choosing projects based on his passion. He said that the best advice he could offer an aspiring writer would be to *live simply*. If you want to be happy as a professional writer, you'll want the luxury of choosing projects you believe in instead of being forced to take projects to pay the mortgage.

It's the Presentation, Dorothy

The surest sign of an amateur is a spiral-bound script with a fancy cover. Keep it simple when showing a script around to a representative. Most people don't even want a printed script any more; they will just ask for it submitted as a PDF e-mail attachment. However, when a printed script is requested, use a plain cardstock cover page with just the necessary info: title, name, date, Writers Guild of America registration number, and address. Three-hole punch. Three brass round-headed fasteners. And please, keep it more than eighty-five pages and fewer than 120.

There's More to Life than Rejection

Most likely, your script will get rejected. I am not trying to be negative; I am merely espousing a reality of this business. For most of us screenwriting mortals, there will be *lots* of rejection, and times when it gets so bad you'll want to stay in bed for days, draw the curtains, and weep.

Don't worry; this is normal. There is not much else to say. Be open to your growth. Enjoy the daily process. By now you should see that rejection is good. Or, at least a necessary part of your growth as a writer and a human being.

Enjoy the Journey

The fact that you are not rich and famous yet is good. Yes, really. See rejection not as a snuffing out of your soul, but as a rebirth, a gift that forces you to change, to learn, to grow. It is merely the world saying to you, "Sorry, but we will not let you in the door until you are ready. And based upon what we have just read, you are not ready. Don't be mad at us, but thank us, because when we finally do let you in, you will be ready to enter."

THE REJECTION HALL OF FAME

If you've tried, really tried to see rejection as something good, yet you've failed and are close to the edge of depression, there's one last little trick that might help: build a Rejection Hall of Fame. As a young writer, I was rejected on hundreds of occasions (at last count). At first, I was miserable, but then I made a conscious choice to embrace rejection by pinning up all my rejection letters (back then, there was no e-mail) in the hallway entrance to my apartment, creating my own personal Rejection Hall of Fame through which all had to pass to get inside. Soon I, and all my family and friends, was inured to all the rejections. They no longer held sway over me. In publicly sharing my rejections, I took the devil in my arms, we became fast friends, and my colleagues marveled at my tenacity.

This is an appeal for you to NOT take a short-sighted approach to life, art, and screenwriting, and to take the long view. Enjoy the process of writing and rewriting. And don't be so hard on yourself.

From: "Dorothy" <WannaBeScribe@netmail.net>
To: "Oz" <OzProf@earthmail.com>
Subject: A basin of liars

Dear Prof. Oz:

I'm glad we're friends again, but I have to be honest with you here; this whole writing thing seems way too structured and limiting for me. I've come to believe that Hollywood's a basin of liars filled with plastic, superficial people I can't relate to. I want to spread my wings, soar with poetic language, rise above the hypocrisy of La-La Land. I want to have the freedom to write scenes that last more than a page. I want to create fully realized dramatic moments filled with real three-dimensional human beings, not just two-dimensional characters.

In other words, no agents, managers, or producers will return my calls or e-mails. I'm ready to quit and sell shoes. Thoughts?

Best,
Depressed as Hell

P.S. Have you heard good things of Zoloft?

CHAPTER 12

The Writing Life in Oz

But Dorothy found she was riding quite easily.

"Quick, Dorothy!" she screamed. "Run for the cellar!"

Toto jumped out of Dorothy's arms and hid under the bed, and the girl started to get him. Aunt Em, badly frightened, threw open the trap door in the floor and climbed down the ladder into the small, dark hole. Dorothy caught Toto at last and started to follow her aunt. When she was halfway across the room there came a great shriek from the wind, and the house shook so hard that she lost her footing and sat down suddenly upon the floor.

Then a strange thing happened.

The house whirled around two or three times and rose slowly through the air. Dorothy felt as if she were going up in a balloon.

The north and south winds met where the house stood, and made it the exact center of the cyclone. In the middle of a cyclone the air is generally still, but the great pressure of the wind on every side of the house raised it up higher and higher, until it was at the very top of the cyclone; and there it remained and was carried miles and miles away as easily as you could carry a feather.

It was very dark, and the wind howled horribly around her, but Dorothy found she was riding quite easily. After the first few whirls around, and one other time when the house tipped badly, she felt as if she were being rocked gently, like a baby in a cradle.

—L. FRANK BAUM, *THE WONDERFUL WIZARD OF OZ*

From: "Oz" <OzProf@earthmail.com>
To: "Dorothy" <WannaBeScribe@netmail.net>
Subject: Life is suffering

Dear Depressed:

Enough whining! Sit up straight and listen. Zoloft is not the answer. Ben & Jerry's might work for a few minutes, but a more permanent solution is what's necessary. So try this:

Get a routine. Commit to writing every day for the same amount of time. Prioritize your life around your writing. Load up iTunes with Dylan and whatever other music inspires you. Crack open a cold Coke Zero and focus on the art form.

I tell my students that if they can write one good scene a day, or even one good line, then at least their lives have some semblance of meaning.

There's no clean and easy way to become a writer; just keep plugging away and avoid hitting the sauce. It'll happen for you, trust me.

Before you go off half-cocked, and start medicating yourself with anti-depressants, please, lie down, pull up your down-filled comforter and listen up—it's storytime.

Oy vey,
Rabbi Oz

The Rabbi of Oz

There is a little known Yiddishe version of *The Wizard of Oz* I would like to share with you now. Pay attention, bubbeleh.

A little old rabbi in eastern Europe was plagued with a recurring dream about a great treasure buried under a bridge near the king's palace. One day, the village's synagogue burned down and the townspeople desperately needed money to rebuild it. So the rabbi set out to find the buried treasure under the king's bridge. (Please note, since this story takes place before TV existed, people gave more credence to dreams than they do today.)

The rabbi traveled for days until he finally reached the bridge from his dreams. When he got there, he was told by one of the king's guards that it was against the law to dig on the king's property. The rabbi and the guard argued and since the rabbi was very good at talking (as most rabbis are), the guard soon felt comfortable with him and revealed that he, too, had been plagued by a recurring dream. However, in his dream, the great treasure was not buried under the king's bridge, but hidden under the stove in a poor old rabbi's house way out in the country. "Ah-hah," said the rabbi, hugged the guard, and scampered back home. Sure enough, when the rabbi started digging under his stove, he discovered that the treasure he had been searching for was buried in his house the whole time.

The Moral of the Story

Think about it. It was there the whole time. Right under his nose. And so, yes, it is all there for you in L.A. or Topeka or Helsinki, or wherever the heck you are. No matter how far you run, your footprints will always be only one step behind you.

The Cowardly Caged Lion

Sooner or later, you will probably come to the conclusion that you and your writer friends really aren't like other people. I like to think of writers as more like a subculture of Kafkaesque hunger-artists, normal in appearance, but really more like starving, wild-eyed caged lions pacing back and forth.

Yes, writers seem to suffer from something I call the caged lion complex, whereby they spend their life yearning to be set free from their confines to roam the countryside and join the world. But even if they do escape, everybody else is immediately onto them. No matter how hard the lion tries, everybody can tell that the lion doesn't belong; that he isn't fit to mill about among *them*.

So, we cowardly lions, what do we do? Well, we either wander around, day and night, dreaming of being as ignorantly and blissfully happy as *they* are, or else we panic, run back to the zoo, demand to be let back into our cages, and talk of how completely repulsed we are by the very sight of *them*. Either way, there's never any pleasure in life because we're always too busy thinking about the experience and how we're going to write about it.

So, in the end, we give in to the truth that our cage is the only home we will ever have; it is where we truly belong, pacing back and forth, snarling and snapping at anyone who dares ridicule us.

It's Lonely on the Yellow Brick Road

Once you've worn a path into the concrete floor of your cage, you are thinking about picking up and moving someplace new. But moving is not the answer. As I said before, no matter how far you run, your footprints will always be one step behind you, as well as all your psychological baggage. So instead of moving out, get up and look into the mirror.

GETTING A LIFE IN THE EMERALD CITY

Years ago, I had a private student who had been working on her first script for a very long time. She always told me of how she dreamed of selling her screenplay, quitting her bookkeeping job, and becoming a professional writer. Finally, I couldn't help myself. I turned to her and said, "You know, for most people, it takes five to ten scripts (five to ten years, too) before they are writing professional-caliber stuff—and even then, many of them never make it as professional screenwriters."

She looked at me, drew in a deep breath, and said, "I know. And I know I might never sell this. I might never even become a professional writer, and even if I don't, that's okay. I need to write. I love it. It gives me a dream. A life."

So if you ever feel like quitting, if it all feels like a magnificent waste of time and energy, take some time off and ask yourself some questions about your dreams and your life.

- ✧ Do you need to write?
- ✧ Does it make you a better person? A happier person?
- ✧ Does it give you a dream? A life?

If you are still unsure, sit up straight and listen to one last story.

More Light, More Light!

Last year, I went out to the Angeles National Forest to get away. As I was driving around in the pouring rain, I realized it was the first time in ages that I was somewhere without streetlights. It was so dark, so pitch black, that when a car approached from the opposite direction, I was struck by the specter of the other car's halogen lances of light rushing toward me.

This image reminded me of when I was sixteen and first learning to drive. I remember shakily drifting down dark country roads in Connecticut only to be horrified by long white spears of light racing toward me. To pierce me. To crash into me. A head-on collision seemed inevitable. Certain death at a young age. I was willing to die, but first, I wanted to fall in love, at least once.

So I pulled over to the side of the road and let the oncoming traffic pass, while my dumbfounded father asked me, "Hey, you okay?
Why'd you pull over?"

"Dad, they were gonna hit us."

"Ahh. Don't talk crazy!"

"But they were speeding straight at us."

My father touched my hand and said, "Kiddo, take it easy. It just
looks that way. All you gotta do is stay on course. Focus on what's
in front of you, keep moving forward, and stay in your lane."

So I did, and miracle of miracles, I passed the oncoming traffic
without crashing. I cruised forward in my lane and cars ceaselessly
whirred by me in their lane—a good two or three feet separating
us. As I kept driving, I started to trust that others would stay in
their own lanes as long as I stayed in mine. I was learning to believe
in my own power and trust in others . . .

Things looked good. I sped up. No problem. Then suddenly an
oncoming vehicle flickered its brights at me as it passed. What was
I doing wrong? What was going on? Then, I realized that they were
just warning me of a speed trap ahead. I loved the idea that even after
my father finished teaching me to drive and I might be driving all
alone one night, there would always be others around to warn me,
to constantly prove to me that the world can be a hospitable place.

Our planet is large, but it is not inherently threatening; it is
only the nightly news that convinces us so. There are well-meaning
souls everywhere. There are good folks out there who are trying to
protect others and to ease our passage forward. Just stay on course,
trusting, traveling, always driving forward.

There will be times when light from oncoming cars will get in
your eyes, but the glare doesn't have to blind you. It can be soft-
ened with a mere change of mindset. It can be muted into an ally.
It can be transformed into a glowing beacon to guide you on your
way. Trust in the light and the flow of the traffic on the road ahead.
Trust. As you continue to write, you'll see that all the work you are

doing can do only one of two things: shroud your world in darkness, or help you admit more light. So my dearest friend, as Goethe did on his deathbed, choose "More light, more light!"

Move Your Butt, Dorothy

Whatever happens as you keep driving forward, don't blame other people for being different from you and don't blame Hollywood for being Hollywood. It is a shallow, superficial, capitalistic, consumer-driven place, but it cannot be faulted for being itself. Hollywood is not about art, so don't fool yourself and don't blame the denizens of Tinseltown for not being something other than what they are. If you can accept them for who and what they are, then, and only then, should you decide that this is the type of business you want to be in and that these are the types of people you want to play with.

There is nothing wrong with commercial writing as long as you understand and appreciate it for what it is: mere commerce, used-word salesmanship, a means for you to amass wealth without breaking your back, a means to exchange your specific skills for desirable goods and services, nothing more or less. And if this sounds a tad too pragmatic, when you can, slip in a highbrow theme or a smidgen of morality when no one's looking.

THE THREE PS

If your headlights start to fade or your windshield gets blurry, remember the three Ps: Patience, Persistence, and Perseverance.

As Charlie Darwin used to say, "It's dogged that does it." Be dogged; always keep working. Yes, you will get depressed at times. Yes, you will procrastinate. Yes, there will be bad days when all you write seems trite, clichéd, and hackneyed, but it happens to the best of us.

As Smart as the Average Dorothy

Never forget—intelligence is relative. How many Einsteins are there, really? And if everyone were an Einstein, then who'd be left to watch movies? In fact, Einstein became known as Einstein (instead of Bad Haircut Al) only in his later years, once he used his creative intelligence to set himself apart as a scientist.

To set yourself apart, all you need to do is to feel more deeply than the average person, convey that on the page, and be willing to work hard—really, really hard.

The Academia of Writing

There comes a time in every screenwriter's career when she feels the need to cease a solitary existence and enroll in a class or workshop. Before you jump in, be aware that many of these classes are taught by petty people. Of course, not all workshops are evil. In fact, there are many wonderful workshops and teachers across the country. Just make sure that the instructor of your workshop promotes constructive, not destructive, feedback, and the other students seem talented, supportive, and serious.

In the financially strapped academic world, this is no longer the age of tenured, chaired faculty, but that of the journeyman teacher, the part-time writer and part-time lecturer who, like the ancient Greek pedant (note the root *ped*—foot—the teachers of yore traveled on foot), travels from one classroom to another to keep bread on his table.

So, my first word of advice to any potential student is to pick your pedant carefully. There are good ones out there, but many are just doing it for the bread. Usually, you can smell this last type from fifty feet away and you should avoid them. If you're unsure, query them as to whether they're working professionals in their chosen field. If not, there's a good chance they're never-has-beens who want to bring you down before you can achieve more than they did.

WRITE LIKE AN AUTEUR—OR NOT

Study film, and the subject of authorial intent is bound to come up. Are writers and directors consciously trying to make a movie filled with subtle cultural icons, mythological images, and unifying filmic devices—or is it just dumb luck? When we do find evidence of them within the text, what are we to make of it? What the hell's an *auteur* anyway? In truth, how conscious are authors? And if authors are unconscious, doesn't that devalue all their hard work and endow every critic, viewer, and audience member with more power than they deserve? Or even worse, sometime someone will say, "I studied Movie X and found a preponderance of subtextual, postmodern, oedipal, homoerotic elements in it, but then I met the filmmaker and asked him about it and he told me I was crazy, so what's the truth?"

 SOMETIMES A CIGAR . . .

I once attended a screenwriting seminar taught by Jeff Arch, the guy who wrote the original script for *Sleepless in Seattle*. Afterward, I rushed up to him and said, "I read in this scholarly article about your film that within the text of your script, the Empire State Building functions as a rigid, ever-present phallus symbolizing the long, drawn-out sexual tension between the two lovers and their frustrated desire for sexual consummation. Did you have this in mind when you wrote the script?"

At which point, he laughed at me and said, "Sorry, but sometimes the tip of the Empire State Building is just the tip of the Empire State Building."

These are all good questions raised over and over again by my students. The answers are not simple or completely straightforward, but they can and need to be articulated. The French have a theory that has caught on around the world that suggests that the film is so highly influenced by the hand of its director that he becomes labeled as the *auteur* (the author) of the film, even if he is not the writer.

The truth is—we are all, to a certain extent, unconscious creatures. No matter how much we try to convey certain story elements, inevitably others will reveal themselves to perceptive critics and audience members. Hence, authorial intent is a valid, significant factor but far from the final word in any analysis of a filmic text. In fact, there is a moment in the film *Annie Hall* that brilliantly illuminates this phenomenon. About thirty minutes into the film, there is a scene in which Alvy Singer (played by Woody Allen) is standing in line to see a movie when a Columbia University film professor right behind him begins conjecturing on Fellini's authorial intent by paraphrasing the great media theoretician, Marshall McLuhan. Alvy gets so annoyed by the professor's pedantic tirade that he reaches behind a nearby curtain and magically pulls out the real Marshall McLuhan, who tells the professor, "You know nothing of my work." This silences the professor and ends any and all debate on McLuhan's authorial intent. Then, Alvy turns to the camera and says, "Boy, if life were only like this!"

Yes, we would all love to be able to pull McLuhan out whenever we need him to support our arguments and end all debate. Unfortunately, real life does not allow this, McLuhan isn't available behind a nearby curtain, and authorial intent is a complex and murky issue. There are, however, ways for authors to empower themselves—without venturing into academia.

Empower Thyself, Wizard!

Many writers like to try to layer their work with as much meaning and as many subtle, esoteric references as possible. If you do that, never lose sight of the fact that all of these things come second, after telling a good story.

If an astute critic notices that in all your work, your characters tend to have passionate love affairs with their mothers, you might head back into therapy or better yet, move out of your parents' house. Either way, learn from the trends in your work, and then move beyond them.

If critics find something significant in your text that endows it with greater import and meaning, agree that you meant to put it there (even if you didn't), and if they insist on taking petty potshots at you that could impair your growth as a writer, ignore them. It is not your concern whether the oedipal impulse shines through clearly; you must concern yourself only with trying to tell the most interesting, original, and vibrant story you can. Period.

A Cautionary Broomstick Tale

In writing classes, there is always the potential for students to become pasteurized, homogenized Robert McKee clones, debilitated by criticism, their hearts set on that just-out-of-reach million-dollar spec script sale. But if you have an awareness of this potential, you will not fall into this trap. Instead, you will take what good you can get out of these classes and devote your energy to working on a new script, or even better yet, achieving a deeper understanding of yourself.

For only through self-knowledge and cognitive development comes growth. I have seen it in my writing classes. Some students, who may be quite talented in their use of the language, write the same stories over and over again, spinning their wheels, never getting beyond writing that is a vainglorious effort to display intelligence. In the end, they only succeed in demonstrating an irritatingly glib and arch persona.

Meanwhile, there's always a quiet young woman in the corner who hasn't spoken much all semester until on the last day she surprises the dickens out of me with an insightful, bold piece of writing even though her first piece of the semester was a trite sci-fi thriller about a bowl of rancid potato salad gone on a rampage. Or better yet, there's that acne-scarred pothead who wrote almost exclusively about giant killer insects all semester long, then finally writes about something real in his own life and he ends up selling his script for a cool million.

That could be you.

From: "Oz" <OzProf@earthmail.com>
To: "Dorothy" <WannaBeScribe@netmail.net>
Subject: Beyond the rainbow

The path itself is the goal, or as Shakespeare said, "The play is the thing." Life happens while you're grappling with becoming someone or something else. So embrace and enjoy the grappling.

All the Ps on Earth,
Oz

P.S. I've also been thinking about some new and creative ways to jump-start your career. I will e-mail you tomorrow with those. So hang on!

CHAPTER 13

Creating Your Own Career, the Indie Way

Don't let them make you into their slave.

The Wicked Witch was both surprised and worried when she saw the mark on Dorothy's forehead, for she knew well that neither the Winged Monkeys nor she, herself, dare hurt the girl in any way. She looked down at Dorothy's feet, and seeing the Silver Shoes, began to tremble with fear, for she knew what a powerful charm belonged to them.

At first the Witch was tempted to run away from Dorothy; but she happened to look into the child's eyes and saw how simple the soul behind them was, and that the little girl did not know of the wonderful power the Silver Shoes gave her.

So the Wicked Witch laughed to herself, and thought, "I can still make her my slave, for she does not know how to use her power."

—L. FRANK BAUM, *THE WONDERFUL WIZARD OF OZ*

From: "Oz" <OzProf@earthmail.com>
To: "Dorothy" <WannaBeScribe@netmail.net>
Subject: Making it happen . . .

Dearest D.:

It is time to start making things happen with what you've written. Hey, if things ain't going your way, do something about it. Now I'll tell you how to get a career off the ground on your own.

Remember, you can't control the rain, but you sure as heck can control whether you get wet. So go put your raincoat on and let's go for a stroll in the rain.

Enough said. Go forth and make your dream happen.

Love and Potato Knishes,
Ozzie

Write a Low-Budget Script that You Can Direct

If you are really a screenwriter, it shouldn't be too difficult for you to think about a concept that can be done on a low budget. Think claustrophobia here. What I mean is that if you can think of a great idea that works in one single location, you have an instant low-budget classic.

For inspiration, you might want to look at stage classics that work such as *12 Angry Men,* in which there is great drama for more than two hours as twelve men on a jury try to determine the fate of an accused man on trial. The brilliance of this conceit is that it can all be done on one set and it does not feel false. The fewer the sets, the fewer the actors, the better.

Create a Kickass Website for Your New Low-Budget Classic

Yes, whether you like it or not, a website is now mandatory. Before you can raise money or move forward on your project, you will need a website that you can drive traffic to for people to learn about and get excited about your project.

Form a Corporation and Create a PPM

Now, take the title of your script and use that title as the basis for the name for a new corporation you can form. This is important since you as an individual artist cannot (nor should you ever) take money from anyone. If you do, you can be legally liable and also subject to lawsuits and lots of legal problems. You'll also need to learn about blue sky laws, which pertain to taking money from investors. Wikipedia.com defines a blue sky law as: "A state law in the United States that regulates the offering and sale of securities to protect the public from fraud. Though the specific provisions of these laws vary among states, they all require the registration of all securities offerings and sales."

To help abide by these laws, once you establish your corporation, you are best served by creating a PPM—a private placement memorandum written by a lawyer. This is a legal document that allows your corporation to take money from investors. It also has lots of clauses in it to protect you and to protect your investors.

For all these matters, please, please, please, consult a good entertainment lawyer who understands the possible legal ramifications.

Create a Trailer and Start Tweeting, Baby

If possible, go out and shoot a scene or two from your film. This should not cost a lot. Once you've edited into a littler trailer (or what is called a sizzle reel in the biz), it can be an essential tool in helping you gain legitimacy and the backing you need. Post your trailer on YouTube and then start Tweeting about it.

There is no guarantee that this will lead to anything, but it can't hurt in your quest to get your project out into the world.

Get Investors

If you have all your ducks in a row—you have done your due diligence, you have a great script, you've created a rock-solid corporate entity and PPM, and you've shot a great sizzle reel—you need to get some moola. Fortunately, there are many ways to do this today. In the old days, you had to go beg and plead and borrow from family and friends. Of course, this is still a viable option, but today there are a lot of other alternatives as well. First, you might consider trying to reap some funds from those 600 Facebook friends that you have.

If that doesn't work, try sites like *www.IndieGoGo.com* that allow you to post your trailer, tell the world what kind of film you want to make, and pray that some moola will come your way. You can also check out sites like *www.ArtistShare.com,* which serve as a portal to raise capital. Of course, in exchange for this moola, you might have to give something to your investors—a chance to be an extra in your film, a credit, a special thanks at the end of the film's credit roll, a signed DVD, a seat at the world premiere, etc.

In addition, there are a multitude of fundraising platforms that can handle donations online. Some only allow nonprofit organizations to use their services, so read the fine print. Several group fundraising services allow you to collect donations right on your website or on their website. For example, ChipIn.com is a micro-funding site through which supporters can give as little as 25 cents and it collects your funds via PayPal. TipJoy.com is another micro-funding site through which supporters can give via Twitter and it collect your funds via PayPal. Fundable.com is different from the other services since it promises that your project will be funded only once pledges meet your stated dollar goal. There are a bunch of these types of sites out there, so choose carefully and be careful to note which ones are exclusively for the nonprofit sector.

From: "Dorothy" <WannaBeScribe@netmail.net>
To: "Oz" <OzProf@earthmail.com>
Subject: Got my raincoat, but . . .

Dearest Corporate Wizard:
I am inspired to take action, so here's what I'm in the process of doing:

1. I have formed a writer's group of like-minded screenwriters. We are not associated with any university and nobody is paying for the class or getting academic credit. We are just people who love screenwriting and want to improve our skill sets. And, we have only one rule, "You must engage in constructive, not destructive, criticism." We meet once a week and every week, we have to send our pages to the rest of the group via e-mail in advance. (FYI, we have called the group The Emerald City Screenwriters.)
2. I have started a screenwriting blog. I don't know how many people read it, but it's good for me to talk about my process, since it forces me to gain a certain degree of consciousness with my writing.
3. I have formed an LLC and have hired a lawyer to help me create a PPM (Private Placement Memorandum) in order to legally raise money for a low-budget film that I have written and want to direct. I figure I can't afford waiting around any longer and I need to make this happen, so I'm

gonna raise the money and do it myself—that is, of course with the help of other people, and their funds . . .

4. I have started a Twitter account, where I will keep everyone abreast of things as they move forward with my low-budget indie film. So you can follow me on Twitter and check out my tweets.

5. In the meantime, with basically no money and everybody working on spec, we've shot a few scenes as sort of test run/trailer—or what we're calling a sizzle reel—that we are putting together in order to help raise funds. In essence, even though it's less than five minutes, the whole project seems more real when we have a bit of it on film, or should I say, video. If you are interested, you can check the sizzle reel out on my Facebook page and, of course, on YouTube. It isn't a perfect trailer, by any means, but it does give you a good sense of my film and I have to say, I think I learned a lot by doing it.

6. Shall I send you the PPM? Would you like to be one of my investors? I think it's a shoe-in to recoup since I am writing a script that can be shot in a short period of time with a limited number of actors and in essentially one location. And most importantly, everybody is essentially working for free and so the budget's miniscule—$20,000 or so . . .

7. You know what, forget about it. I don't want your filthy money. In truth, you've already given me so much I kinda feel bad about even asking. So ignore the previous request and be well.

Your indie acolyte

From: "Oz" <OzProf@earthmail.com>
To: "Dorothy" <WannaBeScribe@netmail.net>
Subject: Good luck, but . . .

Dear Ms. Twitter Blog Acolyte:

I am proud of you, but also glad you did not attach the PPM, since my Alzheimer's hasn't spread so far through all the dendrites in my brain that I would ever consider investing in a film.

With that said, and please forgive me if I sound like a wet blanket here, and yes, I know I was the one who suggested all this indie film low-budget thing, but I'd just like to add that I hope you don't have any false expectations with it all. You see, with the rise of home video technology, every schmuck and his mother are making films and there just is not enough room in the universe for anyone to distribute the majority of these pieces of dreck. Sure, there's the unlimited capability of the Internet, but still even if people can download your film via the Net, do you have the megabucks to publicize the film to drive the awareness that leads to the downloads?

Okay, I'll relax. I'm sure you're aware of all this, but I think it's important that I stress that the majority of these low-budget indie films never get into Sundance and never get distribution and so I need not go on another diatribe. Every year you hear about a kid who spent $1,200 and gets into Sundance, but what you never hear about is the other 10,000 kids who spent millions of their parents' dollars to make crappy indie films that end up being incredibly expensive DVDs that you have to watch when you come over to their homes to visit, since there's no way in Hell these films will ever get distribution.

Sorry, sorry, sorry . . .

Let me reiterate. I do think it's a good idea what you are doing. Even if you end up spending $20,000 on a film that does not recoup or get distribution. Even if it's a total flop, in the end, it's still a whole lot cheaper than film school and I bet you'll learn a whole lot more.

More passion, more patience, and more perseverance.

And of course, keep grappling,
Prof. Oz

From: "Dorothy" <WannaBeScribe@netmail.net>
To: "Oz" <OzProf@earthmail.com>
Subject: Don't bring me down, dude . . .

Dear Mr. Negativity,
Even with my raincoat on, I must ask, do you enjoy raining on people's parades?
I'm trying to spread my wings here and I was hoping to get your support and encouragement, but I guess that's being a bit overly optimistic, especially when dealing with such a cranky old winged monkey.

Yikes and OUCH!
Crushed in the Poppy Field

From: "Oz" <OzProf@earthmail.com>
To: "Dorothy" <WannaBeScribe@netmail.net>
Subject: Mr. Negativity

Hey, sorry, I'm on your side. I really am.
Just trying to be the voice of reason in your life.
I watched your little sizzle reel trailer on YouTube and enjoyed it. So I wish you all the best and hope you can raise enough money to make your movie. Learn as much as you can. I hope you get distribution and get into Sundance and win lots of awards and fulfill all your dreams . . .
And if you don't, I'll still be here for you.
Go forth. Make movies. Prosper.

Yours,
Oz

From: "Dorothy" <WannaBeScribe@netmail.net>
To: "Oz" <OzProf@earthmail.com>
Subject: Sorry, it's been so long since I last wrote

Dearest Oz:

Well, I raised the money from family and friends, made my movie, and have spent months trying to get it into film festivals and all that crap and frankly, I'm sick and tired of it all. Maybe the most important thing I've learned from the whole process is that I don't really want to be a film-maker, I just want to be a screenwriter.

I like sitting in cold, dark holes all day staring at a glowing screen. I hate running around film festivals begging film geeks to go see my movie. I'm sick of trying to get distributors to return a phone call or an e-mail. I'm beat and thoroughly exhausted . . .

Egads,
Indie Filmmaker

P.S. And don't you dare say I told you so.

From: "Oz" <OzProf@earthmail.com>
To: "Dorothy" <WannaBeScribe@netmail.net>
Subject: I'm all aTwitter

Not exactly sure how to respond, but I can honestly say this. I have been enjoying your blog but please never use the word "blogosphere" around me. And yes, I'm one of your followers on Twitter, so I have been keeping abreast of your situation and—well, frankly, I think you are a fantastic failure, in the kindest, gentlest sense of that phrase.

In other words, you are doing it and learning and growing and I think it's all fantastic. Who cares if you don't get a three-picture deal at Paramount after making this film? Who cares if you don't get distribution?

You are doing it. You are in the game. You are learning. You are getting better. I promise you that your next screenplay will be ten times better since you tried being a director and had to deal with all the realities of making a movie. God bless you, dear child.

You are creating light from whence there was only darkness.

Keep moving forward, always forward.

God bless,

Oz

From: "Dorothy" <WannaBeScribe@netmail.net>
To: "Oz" <OzProf@earthmail.com>
Subject: Muchas gracias

Yo Ozzie:

First of all, thanks for the kind words and happy that you're a follower on Twitter (actually, I always thought of you as more of a leader, but still . . .) and welcome to the BLOGOSPHERE!!! (sorry, couldn't help it.)

Okay, seriously now, I've been writing so much recently, I've been remiss in keeping up with the other aspects of my life.

In keeping with your wise words, I've made art out of my suffering and written a little poem. I thought you might get a kick out of it.

How to Be a Screenwriter
Kill your whole family
Or at least disown them.

Write a movie about your parents' divorce
And how they abused you
Sexually and/or emotionally
(before you killed them),
and how you'll never get over it.

(If they didn't get divorced
and/or abuse you,
don't ever tell anyone
and pretend like they did.)

Wear black.

Remember, pain is good.
Find ways to suffer
that look and sound bad
but really aren't.

Don't ever fall in love.
EVER.
Instead, be chaste
and brag about how long it's been.

If you do fall in love,
It must be with someone inaccessible
Who could never love you,
and then write a screenplay about it
Stressing the tragic elements.
Don't forget to fill the pages
with overblown words
From the thesaurus you got for graduation.

If this fails,
Obsess over past relationships
that couldabeen.

Talk about screenwriting
but
Don't really do it.

When you're not talking about screenwriting,
Talk about how much you drink.
Never mention that your gin and tonic
is really just mineral water with a twist.

Xerox every screenplay
you've ever written
For your archives
Which, right now, is an old box
In the basement of your cousin's house
Never look in this box
but feel good about storing your life
In a safe place.

Eat Kraft macaroni and cheese,
Frosted Flakes, vitamin C, Slim-Fast,
Lime green Jell-O, and red gummy bears.

Sleep all the time.
And then, nap in between.

Fantasize about suicide.
Tell everyone
but
know deep down that
it's way too painful
and sloppy so
nap instead.

Avoid other people who wear black
Unless they are as pale as death.
Then talk to them about screenwriting
and drinking and sleeping,

and never ask to see their screenplays,
and never show them yours, either.

Be a semi-finalist in
a small, irrelevant screenwriting contest
that pays you nothing.
Then e-mail your award-winning screenplay
To all the people you hated in your old
stupidgoddamnwritersworkshops.

Don't forget to
Write a poem cynically looking down
upon the writing of screenplays.

Start writing a new screenplay.

There you have it. My first foray into poetry. It's certainly liberating. At least it's short.

I hope you like it. My thoughts are with you,
Poetic Soul

From: "Oz" <OzProf@earthmail.com>
To: "Dorothy" <WannaBeScribe@netmail.net>
Subject: The king of jaded

Dear Literary Lion:

It's good to see that you won't be spending your life wandering the aisles of a bookstore, your mind clouded with puddles of charcoal black espresso, your tongue filled with tales of suffering and woe, your fingers so badly cramped from holding those recycled cardboard coffee sleeves that you fear you may never be able to type again. But let me just say, it is easy to get jaded (and you're talking to the King of Jaded here) and being cynical is not a very becoming quality, especially in someone of your youth.

In the end, I just hope you don't lose the idealism that I so enjoyed. Cynicism is easy; keeping the faith is hard. So please, try to remain one of America's last romantics, for we need you. We need people who have the imagination to foster real change, to make the world a more livable, a mo' better place.

Think about it.

Trying to help,
Oz

From: "Dorothy" <WannaBeScribe@netmail.net>
To: "Oz" <OzProf@earthmail.com>
Subject: WHOOPEE!

Dear Ozzie:

OHMYGOD! You're not gonna believe this, but I got my most recent script optioned. They're not giving me a lot. Well, it's a free option, actually, but still, the producer seems very gung-ho and I think it's really gonna get made. Thanks for your guidance and help. You're the best. Don't worry, when I become rich and famous, I won't forget you.

Love and best fishes,
Hollywood's Hottest Screenwriter

P.S. Oh, yeah—I know what I said a while back about giving up screenplays, and I meant it. So, here's what happened. It's kind of weird. Instead of writing, I've been drinking a lot (that's not the weird part). The weird part is that I was at this bar a few weeks ago and I met someone whose next-door neighbor has a sister who is an assistant to this big independent movie producer and so I gave her my script and next thing I knew, BOOM!

From: "Oz" <OzProf@earthmail.com>
To: "Dorothy" <WannaBeScribe@netmail.net>
Subject: Congrats!

Dearest Wunderkind:
Congratulations and all the best of luck in the film world. I hope your movie wins many awards and you are showered with accolades. Maybe all your hard work has finally paid off.
No matter what, I'm incredibly proud of you.

Your biggest fan,
Prof. Oz

P.S. I want specifics. Write me back and tell me everything.

From: "Dorothy" <WannaBeScribe@netmail.net>
To: "Oz" <OzProf@earthmail.com>
Subject: All the dirty little details . . .

Dear Glinda, The Good Witch:
You want to know everything. Okay, I'll tell you. The so-called big independent producer who optioned my script was a shyster, an alcoholic, a liar, a pedophile, and those are his positive attributes.
Sorry, but I don't want to talk about it, okay?
Either way, thanks for your advice, support, and kindness. You know, now I can honestly say that I no longer feel aspiring or youthful.

Your friend and mine,
Elmira Gulch

P.S. Sorry I haven't written back sooner, but frankly, I'm depressed as hell! Is my career stalling because I don't live in L.A.? In other words, do

I need to live in L.A. to be a real screenwriter? I'd move there, but I've got family and a job here and, well, I can't just up and leave, and, even if I could—the honest truth is I hate L.A.! Do you think this is a problem? Please help!

CHAPTER 14

Sixteen Parting Gifts for the Screenwriter

It doesn't take brains to see that happiness is the best thing in the world.

"The greatest loss I had known was the loss of my heart. While I was in love I was the happiest man on earth; but no one can love who has not a heart, and so I am resolved to ask Oz to give me one. If he does, I will go back to the Munchkin maiden and marry her."

Both Dorothy and the Scarecrow had been greatly interested in the story of the Tin Woodman, and they knew why he was so anxious to get a new heart.

"All the same," said the Scarecrow, "I shall ask for brains instead of a heart; for a fool would not know what to do with a heart if he had one."

"I shall take the heart," returned the Tin Woodman; "for brains do not make one happy, and happiness is the best thing in the world."

—L. FRANK BAUM, *THE WONDERFUL WIZARD OF OZ*

From: "Oz" <OzProf@earthmail.com>
To: "Dorothy" <WannaBeScribe@netmail.net>
Subject: You're a real screenwriter now . . .

Dearest D.:

Well, yes, if you want to come to LA, it will surely help your career, so please do. If not, or if it is too difficult to move right now, you can still create a career from where ever you are.

And in terms of the way you and your script is being treated, I'm sorry. It's actually quite typical, but still, I'm deeply sorry that this is happening to you.

First, let me reassure you that this too shall pass and you will survive and actually grow as a result of this seemingly incomprehensible roadblock in your career. And second, what you need to see is that what is happening is not a curse, but a gift. I'm sure you do not see it that way now, but sometimes you need to look below the surface to see what's really going on. This searching will force you to re-evaluate the nature of your writing, your life, and your soul. In other words, your wish has been granted; you're finally living the life of a professional writer. So, how the hell does it feel, huh?

Just because your script didn't get made doesn't mean you have to give it all up. Heck, what if it were made and the reviews were bad or it was a box office failure? Neither of these would make *you* a failure as a person or as a writer.

Trust me, all the crap you're going through right now can only make you a better writer and a stronger person. Don't fret; just find the blessing in this curse. I've seen the sparks in your smiling prose and I know you can rise above the fray.

Your gifts are solid and your soul is strong and true. Obey its voice and rise above the herd.

My advice, buy a bottle of champagne and celebrate. All is good . . . Or at least, all is how it is meant to be.

And note that your greatest happiness only comes from writing. So at least for now, forget all that other stuff and focus on what really counts—your writing.

Party on,
Oz

Moving Forward into a Career

Once you've become a screenwriter, the choices you make might be even more important than those that you made as a struggling artist. So let's go back to the beginning. Who are you writing for? Why are you writing and what does it all mean in the end? Is it just a job? If you are one of the lucky ones who can write full time, are you really cut out for that kind of life? Do you need another job where you aren't alone all day?

Your next script has to be better than the last. What direction do you want to take with it?

Like our characters in our scripts, we are all shaped by the choices we make.

And in the end, we shall all be judged not by how much money we sell our writing for, but what we do after we make the money. I'm not talking about charity, although that's a very nice gesture. I'm talking about the basic question: Are you still writing? What kind of projects are you writing? What kind of person are you becoming? For when all is said and done, you cannot control how your movie will come out; but if you grow, if you learn, if you change as a result of the process, it is all worthwhile.

Be Pure in Your Love for Writing

Everything you need to know about life, you can learn by living, reading great writing, and writing well. That is all and that is more than enough.

Keep in mind that getting produced and going to a screening are merely the blink of an eye, a few hours of your life and then, snap, it'll all be over and you're in for a great fall if you don't have any plans for the after party.

Most of life never lives up to one's expectations. Like the hardworking college student who looks around at his or her graduation ceremony and says, "What the hell do I do now? For years, I couldn't wait to graduate. Now what?"

But it doesn't have to be that way. In the end, it is the writing itself that must suffice, for the shower of sparks falling from your ascending star is ephemeral, but the legacy of your writing can leave a bright light that burns eternally.

You must continue to work and grow. Your greatest pleasures should come not from rubbing shoulders with celebrities but from creating a great twist, a wonderful character, or a fantastic climax. Live in the writing itself, in the joy of creation, not in the heat of a spotlight that will surely scorch your buttocks.

 # THE SECRET TO SCREENWRITING (AND LIFE)

Remember, we are here on this earth to discover the gifts that God endowed us with, and we only find meaning in life when we return those gifts to the world.

SCREENWRITERS WRITE

Keep putting your stuff out there and then write some more. Do what you need to do for your own sanity and happiness. Care about what others think, but don't be a slave to their opinions, because no matter what they say, it is your piece, not theirs. Go back to your computer and sit, bathed in its phosphorescent glow, safe and happy doing what you love. Write and that is enough.

To Live and Prosper in L.A.

And, yes, if you are serious about screenwriting, living in L.A. is pretty helpful. It is hard for agents and the like to take you seriously if you are not local; however, many people have sold a script from Bumluck, USA and then, and only then, moved to L.A., established themselves, and moved away.

Have you heard of Todd Solondz, the young writer/director who had every screenwriter's dream come true—a signed, three-picture development deal? He hated L.A., gave it all up, escaped back to his childhood home in New Jersey, and got a real job. The weird part of this story is that out of this prodigal son's return to the suburban heartland just off the Jersey Pike, we've been graced with one of my all-time faves, *Welcome to the Dollhouse*, a rare breed of film that is unrelentingly brutal and wonderfully funny.

Sixteen Parting Gifts for the Screenwriter

The Lakota Sioux Indians judged the greatness of people not by the extent of their accumulated wealth but by the magnitude of their gift giving. So I want to give to you, my screenwriting friends, the greatest parting gifts I can think of. May they support you through the long nights, the bad reviews, the endless rewrites, and the questioning of self and skill as you make your way down the yellow brick road.

GIFT #1: We are all screenwriters.

We are all creative individuals. We are all artists. Poets. The nature of language is inherently symbolic, representative. The letters K-E-Y-B-O-A-R-D do not equal the glorious black plastic object I am now banging away on. The word "keyboard" is merely a metaphor, a symbol of the real object that we have come to know as a keyboard. We live in a world of metaphors, a never-ending swirl of poetry. Embrace the poetic. Never lose your love for the lavender-sweet smell of nouns and the salty crunch of adverbs.

GIFT #2: Keep rewriting.

Most of us don't get things right the first time around. Don't fret; you can rewrite your life as many times as you need to until you're happy with it. Like your main characters, you always need to be growing, changing, developing. So, don't fear change, embrace it. Be like The Flying Wallendas—a family of trapeze artists who performed all over the world without a net. Fathers and daughters, mothers and sons, always there to protect each other, to catch each other, to support each other. Like the Wallendas, you need a family, some type of writing group or circle of friends who will be there to support you if you start to fall. Armed with this support, go out there and walk the tightrope of life without a net. Do not fear challenges; instead, fear safety, security, and stagnation. And always remember what Karl Wallenda said, "Being on the tightrope is living; everything else is waiting."

So how do you go about becoming an official Flying Wallenda? The answer is simple. First, keep your mind wide open. Most of the evil in the world originates from ignorance and narrow-mindedness. Be broad in your thoughts, be accepting. Be like the reed at the water's edge, bend with the winds, be sensitive to the world, but never let the bums break you. You'll see that if you keep a window open, even on the coldest days of winter, you might get a bit chilly, but if you're freezing, at least you know that you're alive! Right? RIGHT?

GIFT #3: Create the rules for your world.

As a writer, you can write anything, as long as you clarify and fully understand the rules of the world that you are creating. So create the rules of your world and then live by them. Faithfully. Fully. Joyfully.

GIFT #4: Don't give up, no matter how many drafts it takes.

Yes. Life is hard. Sometimes things don't go your way. Don't pull out an Uzi and blow away your classmates. Start a new project. Keep writing. You are a writer and no one can take that away from you.

GIFT #5: Enjoy writing a good sentence or scene.

Take pleasure in the simple things and small moments in life. Remember, so-called progress is not necessarily a positive thing and all technology is not inherently good. Yes, you can always e-mail or text someone, but how about walking over and interfacing—whoops, I mean, *conversing*—with a real live person face-to-face? Yes, I know it sounds weird, but talking has been a successful means of communication for thousands of years.

GIFT #6: Floss.

GIFT #7: Don't forget to throw in a little comedy.

There's already more than enough drama and tragedy in most people's daily existence. So, try to make people laugh and always be willing to laugh at yourself. Believe me, if you've ever really looked at yourself, you have to admit, you're pretty funny looking. And, it's been scientifically proven that laughter will make you live longer. So, as Steve Martin said, "Be thankful for laughter, except when milk comes out of your nose."

GIFT #8: The audience must care for your main character, and that only happens if *you* care.

In life, as in your art, try to be compassionate. Forgive others and, more importantly, forgive yourself. Life is too short to go through it angry. Try to overlook the faults and negative traits of others. Yes, other people are flawed and insecure, but so are you. Get a new hobby, and move on. Meanwhile, rejoice in the passion and beauty of others.

GIFT #9: Never look down upon others—whether they are fictional characters or real people.

Do not judge people based upon their profession and/or social class. Find the humanity in everyone. Treat everyone as if they have something to offer and what you may find out is that many of them do. Smile a lot at strangers and see how it freaks them out. After you've asked someone how they are, take the time to listen to their response. Talk to your waiter, your mail carrier, your supermarket cashier. When you speak to them, make eye contact and treat them with respect.

GIFT #10: Don't hand over your script too soon.

I know it's tempting, but you only get one chance to make a first impression, so make it a lasting and positive one. (Especially in the film business, where your script will be read by a reader and then that reader's critique will be entered into their production company's computer records, where it will remain, seemingly forever, no matter how many times you rewrite it. The only way around this is to resubmit a new draft under a new name, but even this doesn't always work.) So, no matter what, don't rush things. Take your time. Beware of settling for second best. Beware of settling down. Beware of settling. Resist our conformist market-driven American pack-culture mentality that suffocates the creative instincts and diversity of unique individuals. Don't run with the wolves if you were meant to stroll with the turtles or fly with the falcons.

GIFT #11: Expect to fail.

Yes, once you have waited a certain period of time (see Gift #10), you will have to hand your script over to other people, and there is a good chance that it will be rejected. That's okay. Go ahead. Fail. Yes, you heard me, fail! Take chances and be prepared to fail. It's okay. Happens to the best of us. The only thing that differentiates winners and losers is that after they fail, losers give up and winners try again and again and again. Ted Williams, who many consider to be the greatest baseball hitter of all time, had a batting average of slightly over .400 during his finest season. This, one of the greatest achievements in all of sports history, means that six out of ten times that he got up to the plate, he failed to get a hit. He failed more than half the time—and this failure comes from a man whose batting average was the highest ever.

So remember, there will be times when you fail and you are rejected—both personally and professionally. Don't worry! A little rejection is good for the soul. Embrace rejection. Use it to push yourself to achieve greater things. Remember, there are no wrong choices. Failures are merely learning experiences that help us to get where we need to go.

GIFT #12: Remember: What you write can and will have ramifications.

Be careful of stereotypes, false characterizations, and clichés. Always be aware of the ramifications of your actions and take responsibility for them. As our society grows more and more bizarre, there is a natural tendency to turn inward. Resist it.

GIFT #13: If a scene or a line feels false, weird, or wrong, it probably is.

When in doubt, respect that doubt—whether that means removing a scene that you fear might not propel the story forward or removing someone from your life who is not furthering your growth. If something feels wrong, it probably is. If you're still not sure about a scene, revise until you are convinced it is perfect.

GIFT #14: Take the business of show seriously, for no matter how artistic you are, it is still a business.

Nature abhors a vacuum and so there are very few vacuums left today, especially good ones. Hence, there is no room in this world for artists to live in vacuums. You are part of a world that is bigger than your own head and social circle. Deal with it. Stay grounded in a pragmatic worldview, BUT—and this is a big but—realism breeds mediocrity, and I urge you not toward mediocrity but toward greatness. There is a place for realism, but ask anyone who's ever achieved anything of value and they'll tell you to forget the naysayers who are always screaming, "No you can't" and instead listen to that clear, honest voice in your heart that sings out, "Yes I can. YES I CAN!"

GIFT #15: Never lecture, and beware of people who give advice.

GIFT #16: In the end, your characters are determined by the choices they make, just as you are determined by the choices you make.

Thus, you and your characters must both make choices that force growth. Expect very few things, but dream of everything.

From: "Oz" <OzProf@earthmail.com>
To: "Dorothy" <WannaBeScribe@netmail.net>
Subject: In sum

Don't forget to keep your mind open and then, when you become an official Flying Wallenda, you'll never have to look down, you'll never need a net, because you'll be flying through life held aloft by the memory of the Oz who loved you.

As Always I remain,
Your Wizard of Oz

From: "Dorothy" <WannaBeScribe@netmail.net>
To: "Oz" <OzProf@earthmail.com>
Subject: OMG, thanks, thanks, thanks . . .

Dearest Wizard of Oz:
Thanks, your e-mail was amazing and it really helped.
And yes, I am learning to find pleasure in writing a good scene or line of dialogue. I am enjoying engaging in revisions and starting new projects.

I am paying more heed to the process and am becoming less focused on the end result. In other words, I feel lucky to be working as a writer.

I think this is important to stress because I never want to become like one of those well-paid Hollywood actors on talk shows who bellyache about how hard their lives are now that they are well-known celebrities. So, yes, I know, at times, being a creative soul can be hard, but I am grateful for the chance to be living a writer's life.

So, every day, I write. Sometimes I get paid. One day, I might even get produced. Maybe I'll be lauded and maybe I'll be denigrated, but either way, I'm a working writer. I send my stuff out there and I write some more. I do what I need to do for my own sanity and happiness. I care about what others think, but I'm no longer a slave to their opinions, because no matter what they say, when I sit, I am safe and happy doing what I do best. I write, like that Zen monk, I have the moon in my window, and that is enough. More than enough . . .

Feel better,
Your Little Zen Winged Monkey

P.S. Thanks for all your advice about not putting too much pressure on myself. I know one day, one of my movies will get made and when that happens, I know what I'll do—I'll celebrate with you, and when our celebration is over, I'll go home and write some more.

From: "Oz" <OzProf@earthmail.com>
To: "Dorothy" <WannaBeScribe@netmail.net>
Subject: Arc

Dearest Winged Zen Monkey:

I'm so happy to see that you, like all of my favorite characters on the screen, have a true arc. Yes, my little one, it looks like you are finally growing up. It makes me glow with pride.

Keep it up, kiddo.

With love,
Oz

P.S. I would write more or even fly out to visit, but I'm still not feeling any better.

From: "Dorothy" <WannaBeScribe@netmail.net>
To: "Oz" <OzProf@earthmail.com>
Subject: Concerned . . .

Dearest Oz:

I'm really getting worried now. Are you okay? Why are you not getting any better? What are you suffering from? Is there anything I can do?

Can I come by and see you when I'm back in L.A. next week?

I'm going to be there for some meetings and I'd really love to see you. I make a mean chicken soup. We're talking matzo balls the size of small children. Please, talk to me. I want to be there for you the way you've been there for me.

Get well soon. And guess what? A big producer who has an office on the Paramount lot is interested in my new script. So, who knows, maybe this one will be the one that gets made. And then again, maybe not; but that's okay too.

Best fishes,
The Tin Man After He Got a Heart

From: "Oz" <OzProf@earthmail.com>
To: "Dorothy" <WannaBeScribe@netmail.net>
Subject: Falling with style . . .

Dearest Tin Man,
Would have written back sooner, but still a bit sniffly.
Thank you so much for your kind words, but I don't want you to have to worry about me or waste your time stopping by my humble abode. I'm doing fine. Right now, you need to be focusing on your writing. This is an important time for you. What happens to you over the next few years will make all the difference. Don't waste time worrying about a cranky old fart. Remember what they say about what you should do if you see your guru on the road: Kill him!
So get out of your little soup kitchen and get your ass back in front of your computer. Write and that will be the best medicine you could ever give me.
If you feel blocked, look out at the sky or a blade of grass and remember what Gerard Manley Hopkins said: "The world is charged with the grandeur of God, it will flare out like shining from shook foil."
So let your words *flare out like shining from shook foil.*
Most important, while all this is happening to you, enjoy it. Savor every goddamn moment. It is the best time of your career. A time of hope and great expectations. All lies before you and your future looks so bright, I feel like I ought to wear sunglasses.

If I can't make it to the premiere with you, I insist that you take someone else. At my age, I don't even like to buy green bananas.

But I've reached a sort of reconciliation with my own mortality. If we are all born to die, death becomes not a thing to dread, but a democratic concept, universal, an equal opportunity employer.

The hero myth that drives Western culture and films needs to be reevaluated. True courage and real character are found not in how we stand but in how we fall, and what we leave behind after our fall. Let me illustrate with one last film reference. Do you remember the end of the first *Toy Story*? I'm referring to the moment when Buzz Lightyear glides downward, seeming to be flying—really flying, his lifelong dream achieved for the first time—and his pal Woody screams, "Buzz, you're flying!"

Buzz demurs, "I'm not flying, I'm falling—with style."

Buzz demonstrates that we really can't fly, even if there are times when we may give the appearance of full-fledged flight. Perpetual flight is impossible; we always need to come down to Earth to refuel. It is inevitable. Ask any pilot and they will tell you, flying is easy, it's landing that's tricky. We all need to return to the ground, we are all drawn back to the Earth, always falling, down, down until there is nowhere else to go but down.

Thus, we shall always end up being judged not by how we soar through the ozone but by how we land, and what kind of skid marks we've left on the runway.

So, my dear friend, when you fall, fall with style and grace, for all you have left is your fall. And even if you stumble, never be ashamed of trying.

I hope that something of what I have taught you over the years is valuable to you and that you will take some of my words to heart. I have no family and no written record of who I really was—this person whom you have come to know over the course of these e-mails. The Hollywood films I scripted and the Broadway plays I wrote were commercial vehicles that cannot approximate the amorphous shape of my soul.

These e-mails, then, will have to suffice as the most accurate yellow brick road leading to the Emerald City of my heart and soul. They are the closest thing I have to a legacy. Take them as my most heartfelt offering and if my thoughts reverberate with you, teach them to your own students. They are my gift.

Remember then, the only thing that separates good writing from mediocre writing is that good writing has, at its core and in its heart, *love*. Good writers can never sneer at their creations, their characters, their children; like any mother, all you can really do for your children is love them.

There is no room in this world for authors who look down their noses at their characters; forgo the disdain, dear heart, and embrace your characters. Love them, no matter how evil or despicable they may turn out to be. Write with your pen dipped in the inkwell of compassion, and if you do, you too will always be loved. That is all . . .

And that is more than enough.

Zey gezunt,
Your Oz

P.S. Elie Wiesel tells the story of a rabbi in eastern Europe whose people had a major crisis. They turned to him, their leader, and asked him for help. So the rabbi sat down in a meadow outside his little village, lit a fire, and said a special prayer to the Lord. As a result of this, his town and all its people were healed.

In the next generation, another crisis occurred and the townspeople now approached the rabbi's son, who did the same as his father. He went out to the meadow. He did not know the prayer or how to light the fire as his father did, but he prayed, and *voila*, the town's problems were healed.

In the following generation, another crisis occurred and the rabbi's grandson wanted to help, but he didn't even know which meadow to go to, but he did know the story of his grandfather, and you know what? That was enough.

Yes, God made human beings to tell stories. So don't ever stop telling your stories . . . and mine, too.

CHAPTER 15

Epilogue

There really is no place like home.

"This is all true," said Dorothy, "and I am glad I was of use to these good friends. But now that each of them has had what he most desired, and each is happy in having a kingdom to rule beside, I think I should like to go back to Kansas."

"The silver shoes," said the Good Witch, "have wonderful powers. And one of the most curious things about them is that they can carry you to any place in the world in three steps, and each step will be made in the wink of an eye. All you have to do is to knock the heels together three times and command the shoes to carry you wherever you wish to go."

"If that is so," said the child, joyfully, "I will ask them to carry me back to Kansas at once."

She threw her arms around the Lion's neck and kissed him, patting his big head tenderly. Then she kissed the Tin Woodman, what was weeping in a way most dangerous to his joints. But she hugged the soft, stuffed body of the Scarecrow in her arms instead of kissing his painted face, and found she was crying herself at this sorrowful parting from her loving comrades.

Glinda the Good stepped down from her ruby throne to give the little girl a good-bye kiss, and Dorothy thanked her for all the kindness she had shown to her friends and herself.

Dorothy now took Toto up solemnly in her arms, and having said one last good-bye she clapped the heels of her shoes together three times, saying,

"Take me home to Aunt Em."

—L. FRANK BAUM, *THE WONDERFUL WIZARD OF OZ*

Note to Reader: The following is the text of the eulogy delivered at the memorial service for the man known as Oz.

Dear Friends:

For the next few minutes, I will try to do my best to express to you how I felt about my mentor, my Prof., my Oz. First of all, I'd just like to assure everyone here today that his dog, Meshugeneh, is fine and living with me now. Also, please excuse me—I'm a writer, not an actor, so I'm not used to doing this kind of thing, especially in front of so many people. And, well, revealing my emotions has never been my forte.

But I'd like to try to do justice to a man who changed my life. Ours was an unconventional relationship, based on a love of language, writing, movies, and theater. In fact, we never met face to face.

Regardless, I feel fortunate to have been able to know my mentor through his e-mails. Oh, how I loved his e-mails! Every day, I couldn't wait to get to my computer to see if he had written to me. His e-mails were things of beauty filled with dark fire and raw electricity. Words—beautiful, strong, melodic words—swirled off his pages. I was transfixed. Invigorated. Transformed by his thoughts and lessons. He reached out to me and touched me when I thought no one could. He patted me on the back and caressed my cheeks. He told me I was going to be okay, converted me back into a human being. He made me believe that I counted, that I was worthwhile, good, and important. I wanted to stay in the presence of his e-mails forever.

Yes, I admit it—over the course of our correspondence, I came to love my professor, but who wouldn't have fallen in love with someone who brings a few rays of love and light into this world of darkness and hatred; who wouldn't rejoice in the purity of souls touching and connecting?

For more than six years, we sent e-mails back and forth. I trace my growth by the path of these e-mails, and I attribute everything I have ever achieved as a writer to his tutelage. And now, today, I want to tell you a little bit about the legacy that he left me.

He spoke of change as being the primary factor in a successful story, but my Prof. taught me that it is not merely change or courage, it is more; it is obsession and beyond. Yes, all great stories have one thing in common: characters who are driven beyond obsession, who love more deeply than us ordinary folks, who fight harder, and hold on longer. Characters who are beyond obsession shed light on our lives, they teach us how to live, inspire us to be extraordinary, to transcend the security of narrow-mindedness, and to always and forever strive to become better.

After years of receiving loving guidance from my Prof., I see today as my first chance to start giving something back, to help him finally finish reaping the fruits that he planted. But exactly how would he want me to do this?

And then, I thought of the legends and myths of other cultures that we discussed, especially those of the Lakota Sioux Indians, who judged the greatness of others not by the extent of their accumulated wealth but by the magnitude of their gift-giving.

So as we now say good-bye to the man I knew as the Great and Terrible Oz, I want to give back to you the greatest gift I can think of: Oz's blessing. I was fortunate to have had his blessing bestowed upon me and I want to share it with you. Oz always made me feel safe, gifted, and proud to be his student and a writer. Now I would like to extend his blessing to all of you, as well . . .

Pay Attention to That Man
Behind the Curtain (An Elegy)

You were my Wizard of Oz,
The man behind the curtain
The humbug behind the screen
And when you finally revealed
Yourself
You were no humbug,
No false wizard
But a real mensch,
A real inspiration,
A real kind, loving soul.

You showed me the golden rule of change,
How we are most moved by human transformation.

Your words and teaching changed me,
They showed me that I could get a
Diploma and a medal of valor and a heart-shaped token
But none of those things really matter,
For it is only by going down the yellow brick road,
By going on a long journey with friends,
That one can truly develop the important gifts of
brains and courage and heart.

And then you showed me that the greatest gift you can give
is your blessing
and you blessed us all with your life,
you words,
your thoughts,
your wisdom,
your kindness,
and your love.

And so now, in return, take a small gift from us,
receive our blessing—
Zey gezunt, my Prof., my Oz
Because of you
we will never stop writing,
we will never stop trying to effect change,
we will never settle for anything less.
We will always keep our minds open,
our eyes clear and our voices pure.

Whenever a good story is well told,
we will always hear your voice.
Whenever we look at a blank page,
we will always see your writing.
Whenever we write a perfect scene,
It will be your advice guiding us,
and when we fall asleep at night and dream,
you shall be there once again,
in flames and smoke, bigger than life,
deep in the heart of an Emerald City
waiting to give us more guidance . . .

And if it's true what the Wizard said, that
A heart is not judged by how much you love,
but by how much you are loved by others,
than you can rest assured that many loved you
very, very much . . .

Afterword

Years ago, when I picked up a copy of Richard Krevolin's first book, *Screenwriting from the Soul*, I was transfixed by it.

Let me paint the picture for you. I was a young and excitable boy living in Mumbai, India. I found the book in a bookshop and had to have it. I was reading everything I could get my hands on about writing and wanted to master this difficult art form, not just script-writing, but all forms of writing. Krevolin's voice seemed to speak directly to me and I heard it more clearly than the other voices in the other writing books I had picked up.

Yes, I was just beginning to take baby steps as a writer when, fortunately, his book opened up new vistas for me. It inspired me and led me forward on my journey as I grew to become an established, award-winning screenplay writer in India—where more movies are produced than anywhere else in the world.

After reading his book, I reached out via e-mail and contacted him. We corresponded back and forth over the years and his guidance has been instrumental in my development as a screenwriter and a human being. Who knew I would become a successful screenplay writer? I didn't. Perhaps he did, when he took to me; willing to guide me through our exchange of e-mails in the nascent years of the information age.

Richard has always been a writer who is not boring to read. His writing was always my model for clarity and crispness. He never wrote florid prose or used twelve words when three would do. Chatty, irreverent, entertaining, and with an emotional hook, his writing reached out to me on many levels.

Over the course of our e-mails, we graduated from master and student to equals and friends. We could sense that gradual change even in our exchange of e-mails—at the start, I was an irritable wannabe trying to curry favors with him and learn as quickly as possible. As the years passed, our exchange of e-mails developed into something that was not so much concerned with the techniques of writing as it was with our shared philosophy of life.

And thankfully, upon reading of *Screenwriting in the Land of Oz*, I realized that Richard's gift for writing well and wisely is, thankfully, still intact.

In addition, I'm also happy to report that after many years of e-mail correspondence, last year, Richard found himself in India as a guest lecture for a special writer's conclave he had been invited to. He had a busy schedule, but we made it a point to meet up. After years of correspondence, we finally got to meet in person. It was a surreal experience. Here was the man I had idolized from a million miles away, sitting across the table from me at my favorite local coffee shop. It was a truly awesome experience!

When he asked me to write the afterword for this book, it was as if we had come full circle. And once I read this book, I realized how it partly reflects our story. In a way, I saw the voices of Dorothy as a reflection of my voice and Oz's voice as a reflection of Richard's over the years as we corresponded with each other. From scripting to promoting, from writing for yourself to getting an audience, from Emerald City to Mumbai City, it's all there.

As his first book did so many years ago to me, I hope this book inspires you to discover the fresh and original tale that exists inside of yourself, become a better screenwriter—and maybe, even a better person.

Mushtaq Shiekh
Mumbai, India

APPENDIX A

Contact the Author

Dear Reader:

Unlike Prof. Oz, I'd be happy to hear from you. You can reach me via e-mail at *RKrevolin@yahoo.com* or you can visit my website, *www.ProfK.com*.

Passion, patience, and perseverance—that is all and that is more than enough.

Thanks, and write well, write fast, and write hard!!!

Richard Krevolin

APPENDIX B

Bibliography

Diane Ackerman, *A Natural History of the Senses*, New York, Vintage Books, 1990.

Diane Ackerman, *A Natural History of Love*, New York, Vintage Books, 1994.

Woody Allen, *Without Feathers*, New York, Ballantine Books, 1990.

Aristotle, *Poetics*, translated by Gerald F. Else, Ann Arbor, The University of Michigan Press, 1967.

Peter Brook, *Reading for the Plot*, Cambridge, MA, Harvard University Press, 1984.

Charles Bukowski, *Run with the Hunted*, New York, Harper Collins, 1993.

Don Delillo, *White Noise*, New York, Penguin Books, 1986.

Annie Dillard, *The Writing Life*, New York, Harper Perennial, 1989.

Lajos Egris, *Art of Dramatic Structure*, New York, Simon & Schuster, 1960.

Viktor Frankl, *Man's Search for Meaning*, Boston, Beacon Press, 1962.

Syd Field, *Screenplay*, New York, Dell Trade, 1982.

Sigmund Freud, *Beyond the Pleasure Principle*, New York, Avon Books, 1965.

Gardner, John, *On Moral Fiction*, New York, Basic Books, 1977.

Gardner, John, *The Art of Fiction*, New York, Alfred A. Knopf, 1983.

Harold C. Goddard, *The Meaning of Shakespeare*, vols. 1 and 2, Chicago, Phoenix Books, 1951.

Michael Hauge, *Writing Screenplays That Sell*, New York, Harper Perennial, 1991.

James Hillman, *The Soul's Code*, New York, Warner Books, 1996.

David Howard and Edward Mabley, *The Tools of Screenwriting*, New York, St. Martin's Press, 1993.

Sam Keen, *To a Dancing God*, San Francisco, Harper & Row, 1990.

Annie LaMott, *Bird by Bird*, New York, Doubleday, 1994.

John Howard Lawson, *Theory and Technique of Playwriting*, New York, Hill and Wang, 1960.

Arnold Ludwig, *Price of Greatness: Resolving the Creativity and Madness Controversy*, New York, The Guilford Press, 1995.

Gerald Mast and Marshall Cohen, *Film Theory and Criticism*, New York, Oxford University Press, 1985.

Robert Ray, *A Certain Tendency of the Hollywood Cinema*, New Jersey, Princeton University Press, 1985.

Rainer Maria Rilke, *Letters to a Young Poet*, translated by M.D. Herter Norton, New York, W.W. Norton, 1962.

Linda Seger, *Making a Good Script Great*, New York, Dodd, Mead & Company, 1987.

Preston Sturges, *Five Screenplays*, edited by Brian Henderson, Berkeley, University of California Press, 1986.

Richard Walter, *Screenwriting*, New York, Plume Books, 1988.

Will Wright, *Sixguns and Society*, Berkeley, University of California Press, 1977.

Christopher Vogler, *The Writer's Journey*, Studio City, CA, Michael Wiese Productions, 1992.

Index

About the Author

Richard Krevolin is an author, playwright, screenwriter, and professor. A graduate of Yale University, Richard went on to earn a master's degree in screenwriting at UCLA's School of Cinema-Television, and a master's degree in playwriting and fiction from USC.

For fifteen years, he was an adjunct professor of screenwriting at USC School of Cinema/TV. He has also been an adjunct professor at UCLA Film School, Pepperdine; Ithaca College; and the University of Georgia. Under his guidance, his students have sold film scripts and TV shows to Universal, Sony-Tri-Star, WB, Paramount, Dreamworks, and numerous other studios and production companies.

He is the author of the books *Screenwriting from the Soul* (St. Martin's Press), *Pilot Your* Life (Prentice-Hall), and *How to Adapt Anything into a Screenplay* (Wiley & Sons). He is also the author of several young adult novels and more than twenty stage plays. Krevolin has several scripts in development in Hollywood, including *SAFER* with Tom DeSanto Productions (*X-Men, Transformers*). He was also one of the writers of the documentary, *Fiddler on the Roof: 30 Years of Tradition.* His most recent off-Broadway stage play, *LANSKY*, was nominated for an Outer Critics Circle Award and was a big hit at the National Yiddish Theater in Tel Aviv, Israel. Along with Joseph Bologna, he wrote the stageplay, *Sort of a Love Story,* which stars Bologna and Renée Taylor. This comedy opened in Los Angeles at the El Portal Theatre in 2010 and is now touring the country.

Over the past decade, Prof. Krevolin has flown around the world to teach the art of communication and storytelling to executives, creatives, and brand managers at many different companies including Vaseline, J. Walter Thompson, Ogilvy, Tata Interactive Software, Pond's Skin Care, Panera Bread, Sunsilk Shampoo, Lux Soap, Lifebuoy, and Nike. He has also worked with various top-tier corporate in-house and outside counsel on strategic communication and trial themes for major litigation cases.

Krevolin has been a panelist and keynote speaker at a variety of popular writers' conferences, including the Maui Writers Conference, the Screenwriting Conference in Santa Fe, the Hollywood Film Festival, the Surrey International Writers' Conference, the Kenyan Screenwriters Seminar in Nairobi, and the Hollywood Film School in Kiev, Ukraine. His consulting work has affected hundreds of TV commercials produced all over the world, many of which have won awards including a Golden Lion at Cannes and the People's Choice Award in China. He continues to coach lawyers, writers, and brand executives privately, as well as lecture and lead creative workshops.

For more information, contact him at *www.ProfK.com, www.Power StoryConsulting.com,* or *RKrevolin@yahoo.com.*